ROY CHUBBY BROWN

TELL US ONE WE KNOW

THE AUTOBIOGRAPHY OF ROY CHUBBY BROWN

First published 2015 by DB Publishing, an imprint of JMD Media Ltd, Nottingham, United Kingdom.

ISBN 9781780915081

ROY CHUBBY BROWN

TELL US ONE WE KNOW

The AUTOBIOGRAPHY OF ROY CHUBBY BROWN

With *George Proudman*

DB
PUBLISHING

Contents

Acknowledgements

Chubby Brown has fans and friends all over the world, his stories and memories are here to be read by pal Steven Lloyd and he's said there's so many to thank...

Richie Hoyle, Scotty Owen, Geoff Ormesher, Keith Hammersley, Stuart Littlewood, Nicola, Charlie, Sue from the office. And my rock Helen what a woman !

My inspiration Ken Dodd and more or less every stand up who walks the boards – it's an awkward job but someone had to do it. And of course without the love and support of your family it's not possible. Also thanks to Steve Caron and Simon Hartshorne of JMD Media.

Tar
Chubbys
Xx

Steven Lloyd's thank you
I have been a fan and friend of Roy's for over twenty five years and followed him all over the country. Being from the north east myself I was so lucky to see Roy in his early days learning his craft in the working men's clubs, which alone is one hell of an apprenticeship.
To see Roy now and what he had achieved is amazing. He has amazing talent as a musician a writer a comedian. And I'm honoured to be your friend

Steven lloyd
Roy's publicist

THE GREAT CHUBBY - FOREWORD BY KEN DODD

I've known Chubby Brown since - oh! and even before that! I've worked with him and he is a really good friend, a kind and thoughtful man, a wonderful jovial jolly jester who 'does it his way'.

In the permissive society of today he is an acorn, sorry, an icon of good taste. In his brilliant high fashion patchwork suit and his super smile, he's a true comedy hero. Superstar Chubby! There are many comedians in show business and the magnificent Chubby is right up there with all the greats. A joyful man, a clever man who knows his audience, his customers. He knows they are hungry for laughs and he gives them a good blowout, a banquet of barmyness, a feast of fun for funny folk - Chubby's own special recipes of ribaldry, bed and bawdy!

In his cornucopia of comedy he doesn't do satire, he gives you humour in technicolour, 50 shades of blue! He's like action man, he shoots from the hip or thereabouts. They say he's got charisma, (don't you think it's wonderful that he is still working with this complaint?)

A lifetime of laughter; when he was a small boy at school he spent so much time on the naughty step it raised him up and he discovered he could look through the letter box of life and today he tells it how it is.

Let's hear it for Chubby! Give him a good clap!

Yours truly,
Ken Dodd

INTRODUCTION

Hi everybody thanks for stealing a copy of my new book, it's the fourth in the trilogy, or is it the third? Never was any good at sums, in fact I remember my teacher saying to me, 'Roy,' 'cos that's what they called me back in 1951BC (Before Chubby), she said, 'Roy, if you had ten sweets and I took half of them off you, what would I have?' I said, 'a broken arm, miss!'

Now that paragraph has given you just enough time to get the book back off one of the kids, in case they've picked it up by accident thinking it was *Pepper Pig*, or that I looked like Harry fucking Potter on the front cover; last warning, this book is not for the faint-hearted. I was thinking of using a ghost writer, but I did that last time and at our first meeting I nearly shit myself when he walked straight through the fucking wall instead of entering by the door.

I'd like to say that this book follows on from my previous books, but it doesn't, it's actually a mixture, mishmash, bowl of alphabetti spaghetti, if you like, of unforgettable moments that I completely forgot about until now. By the time you've read this book, there'll be nobody I've had an argument with, slept with or both, that you won't know about, unless of course I don't know about them myself; it was a bit like that back in the 60s and 70s, because in those days you shagged first, and then introduced yourself later, if you could still be arsed. Yes, I'm filling in all the gaps and some of the cracks, no stone will be left unturned, so if something quite random pops up while you're reading, it's because I just remembered it.

They say, 'if you can remember the 60s, then you can't have

been there.' Well, right now I have difficulty just remembering fucking yesterday, and I know I was there, because if I hadn't been I wouldn't be here today, if you know what I mean. So I've compiled a selection of unedited highlights that I've been reminded about from way back when, yes I've delved into the old grey matter to come up with a few stories I don't think you'll have heard before, plus a few stories I don't think I've heard before either, so I'm going to steal a copy of the book for myself. Once you've picked this book up, you just won't be able to put it down, because I've laced it with superglue.

In a few years time, when I'm in the Sea View Nursing Home, I'll probably pick this book off a shelf and think, 'who the fuck's that, how the fuck was he able to squeeze all that into one lifetime, and still get away with it?' I often think that already, and I haven't finished yet, not by a long way. I've had great fun compiling this collection, so please sit back and enjoy the roller-coaster ride back to a time when we watched snooker on black and white television, and didn't learn about the Second World War in history lessons at school, because it was still breaking news. There'll be some of you that will recognise the times I've revisited, when the summers were warmer and the winters were white with snow, then there'll be others that will be thinking, here's another old fogey cracking on about the fucking good old days.

Well, I think I've rabbited on enough, and I'm beginning to bore my fucking self now, so I'll shut the fuck up and let you get on with reading the book. Please enjoy my accumulation of little stories while I'm still around, bless you all for taking the time to go shoplifting, you can always plead mitigation on grounds of insanity if the police catch you, I sincerely hope you'll consider it great value for whatever you paid or didn't pay, whatever the case may be, and once again, many thanks for taking such an interest over the years.

Cheers and happy reading,
Love you all,
Chubbs x

1. 70 Not Out

Would you believe it seventy, never thought I'd get to seventy, I normally get pulled up doing about fifty-five, reading a newspaper while making a telephone call, and they say us blokes can't multitask. Ok so we've started with a laugh at my expense yet again, good to get it over and done with, now let's get down to something more serious. Someone said to me, 'well at least you haven't got dementia,' I said, 'yes, I read about that only the other week, it said that people with dementia are not obese, but I think that's only because they've forgotten where they hid the fucking biscuits.' The thing is, when you get to this age things start to go wrong, a friend of mine. Ted, was given a screening kit from the N.H.S. but he obviously must have misread the leaflet that came with it, because he put some shit in the envelope and sent it back, wouldn't have fancied licking the envelope though, mind you Ted's a schizophrenic, but the positive side is that he's always got someone to talk to.

Now this book is a series of short stories that have happened to me over the years, which I am able to recall whilst going through the ageing process, you see at my age it's easier to remember what happened years ago than it is to remember what happened yesterday, sounds crazy but it's true. There are certain things you have to put up with as you grow older, baldness for starters, the tell tale signs being when you attempt to comb the last four hairs on the right side of your head over to the left side hoping to cover your bald patch, but being careful not to pull another strand out in the process. Yet the only foolproof way to disguise this is by wearing a cap, then if you do get your wardrobe wrong by wearing a polo neck sweater when you've got a bald head, you'll just end up looking like a fucking dick, a circumcised one at that.

The wife said to me, 'I know you might be getting old Roy, but I can still fit into my school uniform,' I said, 'darling, that's because you are only fourteen.' When she found her first grey hair we had tears, it was a bit strange for me too, because instead of staring at a lovely auburn bushy brown bush, I was now looking at one with grey streaks in it, still not complaining though, but it does have the effect of making a happy man feel very old.

You get to an age when every day stuff doesn't really matter, and there'll be times when you pick up the phone after it has rung, and say, 'what do you want, you beady eyed ugly fucking baboon?' because that's what older people tend to say before putting their brain into gear, only to find it's your ninety-year-old mother ringing to see if you're ok. Your sex life becomes none existent, I used to wake up with a 'morning glory' consisting of a proper horn, now it's more like a fucking 'Bendy Bully', you still take Viagra pills, but that's just to make sure you don't piss on your slippers when you go to the toilet, then while trying to get your trousers over your still erect hampton you'll probably put your back out in the process, all the time worrying that if you trip over, you could pole-vault yourself out of the open window. Well some of us might, but just try explaining that one to your neighbour when you land next to him while he's cutting the grass.

You might often smell of dried urine, all the time trying to mask the stink by smothering yourself in Lynx deodorant or Paco Rabanne, then from time to time you'll come up with daft ideas like sewing a hool-a-hoop into your underpants so you can get them on and off easier, just in case you shit yourself; yes I might just apply for the patent on that one.

Getting older does have its advantages though, you can walk straight to the front of the queue at the post office and nobody says anything. A lot of people my age can clean their teeth without having to go to the bathroom, but most of all you can shit yourself in public and everybody says, 'ah, bless him.' So I'm going to say to you all, 'don't be afraid of reaching seventy, embrace it, after all they say it's the new fifty, as I keep telling the police every time they pull me up for speeding, and don't forget, your only ever as old as the woman you feel, and I can confirm that first hand.'

2. When I Was a Kid

was thirteen when dad caught me wanking, well he went absolutely berserk, which I couldn't understand really, because the rest
of the people on the bus just laughed. When I was a kid at school,
there was no such thing as Offstead, nor were there any school gov-
ernors, but our school must have been all right because they said
it was approved. I always thought it was strange when the teacher
joined us in the showers after football, I'd say to Mr Posthlewaite,
'you are a naughty man,' and I once asked him why his willy was
so big, he said, 'it was to hang Mrs Posthlewaite's fanny on,' but
I didn't really understand what he meant, I remember thinking,
'what's a fanny?' It was a rough school but I had Mr Kennedy,
another one of our other teachers, laughing
his goolies off when I met him again years
later; I told him that I'd taught myself to
play the ukulele, drums and the piano, then
I'd written myself some filthy material, so it
appeared I hadn't wasted all that time when
I was at school. What amused him though,
was that most of my material at that time
was about my dysfunctional schooldays.

I'd got my first buzz from comedy when, as
a child, I told my first Fuckerada joke in the
school playground, can't remember where

I'd heard it, but at that age it was probably the most risqué thing ever, all the kids in class wanted to hear me tell it. I can recollect the feeling at the time of telling this mucky joke, getting a laugh, and then wishing I had another joke to tell them, even at that age, once I realised I could make people laugh there was no holding me back. I remember one of my mates asked me if I wanted to go to Sunday school with him, it wasn't really my cup of tea, we didn't go to church, but you got free biscuits, so I went.

During a short break in proceedings, when the biscuits came out, I decided to tell some of the kids my Fuckerada joke, and very quickly a crowd gathered round. By the time one of the adults came over, all these kids were pissing themselves laughing, which prompted this rather authoritarian voice demanding to know what was going on. One of the fucking little wimps blurted out, 'Roy's just told us a Fuckerada joke miss,' well her face went bright crimson, then she grabbed one of my ears and frogmarched me down the hallway and out through the front door, telling me never to darken their doorstep again; it later struck me that I was probably the first and only child ever to have been expelled from fucking Sunday school.

Even in those days I was writing little poems, jotting lines down, not really knowing what I was doing or where it could lead to, but that was the sort of thing you'd keep to yourself at our school, because the likes of Gandy Jarrard or Swett Parfitt would think you were a bit of a cissy boy.

A teacher at our school said, 'today kids, I want you all to explore your inner feelings,' well, we all looked at each other as though to say, 'what the fuck's he on about now?' Probably noticing the blank look on our faces because we were all thick twats, he went on to say, 'I want you to write down a short essay saying how you feel about yourselves, say what you think is wrong or right, what you like or dislike about yourselves, telling it in any way you like. I thought about it for a while, and essay type things weren't really me, but I had been coming up with stuff I could put to rhyme, so I wrote a poem, it went a bit like this:-

Roy, Roy, Roy, have you no shame?
Your fingers are getting tubby; you can hardly write your name.
Just look at the size of you, as you're running down the street,
With your pie and peas, or fish and chips, did your heart just miss a beat?
You'll have to lose some weight son, with the amount of lager you sup;
Stood in front of our old battered oven, shouting 'for fucks sake hurry up!'
You'll have to do something about it, or not for long, you'll be around;
You can't pull young girls' knickers down, if you're six feet underground.

I didn't win the competition with that one, but when it was reported to my father, I did get a fucking big clout around the ear, not the first or the last. I started to put weight on when I was about thirteen, which encouraged dad to come out with one of his favourite lines, 'why don't you get your ears pierced so I can see the fucking telly, Roy?'

I used to pass messages to a girl in school, I remember her

sending me a note saying that she'd lost her virginity the previous night and, as I was a bit naive then, I sent her one back saying, 'never mind, I'll help you find it after school.' One day the teacher caught us and shouted, 'Vasey, stop passing notes,' I said, 'I'm not sir, we're playing cards,' which was ok at our school, as long as it wasn't strip poker during lessons. Yes I was the kind of kid that if the teacher asked, 'right, Royston, you have six sweets and I take three, how many sweets would you have then?' I would say to him, 'six sir, 'cos you're not fucking getting any,' we were all cheeky bastards in our school.

We had a teacher in our school called Mrs Peterson, who would definitely in this day and age be struck off, you see she always wore low cut blouses with short skirts which apparently, you were allowed to do then, and being a secondary modern school, there was so much testosterone flying about that every lad in our class wanted to slip her a length, but we also knew that Mr Hall, the art teacher, had designs on her too. The two of them took our class on a nature walk up Eston Hills, but as soon as we got there they went off together. We didn't know where they'd gone, but there was a derelict building left over from the old iron ore mining days that housed a crushing machine, and from the noise we could hear coming from inside, it sounded like Mr Hall's balls were receiving a right crushing too. It came to me later that he probably only took us up to the old mines so that he could give dick-teasing Mrs Peterson a fucking good old shafting.

MRS PETERSON
Dick Teaser

In the late fifties there wasn't loads to do, so we had to find our own amusement, usually by knocking around street corners up to no good, pinching bottles of milk off our neighbours' steps. I remember there was a health and safety issue, which was unusual for those days, telling us that eating fish and chips would take five years off our lives, and I remember thinking, take them, fucking take them, the smell on its own is good enough for me. Those were the days when you would fart and say proudly, 'that was one of mine,' because then at least your mates knew you were getting something to eat.

For school, I wore a denim jacket with baseball boots and, what I called a cruel pair of trousers at half-mast, which always had the arse hanging out, I think I told everyone at school that there was a nail sticking up on my seat; I would have looked better clothed in a fucking dog's blanket. I remember one teacher's report saying, Roy must try harder just to come to school sometime. You see the only time I liked school was when it was shut, and when I was there the only thing I was good at was drawing cartoons, well drawing anything really.

The truant officer, or Nicker Bobby as we used to call him, was always at our door, because I'd pretend to go to school, and then hide behind one of the buildings near the bins, standing for ages among fag ends, dead spiders, and frozen chips, until I was sure the coast was clear. He caught me in the house one day, but I quickly dived behind the settee when he banged on the door, 'I know you're in there, are you going to answer the door?' I tried to put him off the scent by going, 'meow, meow,' thank goodness my voice hadn't broken yet. 'It's your last chance, or I'll be telling your dad, and then you'll be shouting, 'fucking hell dad, that hurt!" He finished off by shouting through the letter box, 'nice try, young un, but I know you don't have a cat!'

Your life does flash before you when you think you're going to peg it; I thought back to my days at school, which was more like a fucking zoo than a school, I regularly had to bend over to get the cane, which I got so often that my arse was redder than a post office van. Mr Atterton, our headmaster, said, 'Vasey, you keep coming to me because of bad behaviour, the times I've had to use the cane on you, my right arm's getting thicker than my left arm.' But as he wacked me I would sing, *always look on the bright side of life.*' now the Bible tells you to always turn the other cheek, but I don't think it meant when you were having your fucking arse caned, but whatever happened at school, you would never dare go home and tell your father, because you'd just get another clout.

I had no guidance as a child, because dad was always in the pub, and mother had fucked off by then, so I had to amuse myself. For example we had a local shop, and it didn't take me too long to realise that the till was out of sight of the fridge in the corner, so every day I would help myself to lollies and ice cream free gratis, no wonder I'm fucking fat. Some years later, I worked for that same shop delivering newspapers, but on a cold day, I'd walk round the corner and put them all in a dustbin, the shopkeeper was always getting complaints like, 'Alf, we never got our papers today!' I broke down under interrogation, and was sacked on the spot.

Baz, a mate of mine, threw a dustbin through Brown's shop window, just for the hell of it. I'm sure it was nothing to do with the fact that the shop window was full of ladies underwear, testosterone to blame again then. I can't remember what actually happened, but many years later, Baz was telling me about it over a few pints, he said, 'you took all the blame Roy, your dad came round on his bike, and smacked you across the head, but you never said a thing,' then admitted to me saying, 'when I saw your dad flying down the road on his bike, I shit myself, never mind you!'

The sixties arrived and there were flats built with panoramic views that overlooked the slums and the gas works depending on which window you looked out of, it still didn't stop everyone also overlooking their rent though; those flats are still there today, but now full of immigrants, with nothing but a deck chair to sit on. We had some beautiful girls in our neighbourhood, but also plenty who looked like the brides of Frankenstein, and you don't need to be a fucking Oxford graduate to guess which one I married. Our local pub was called the 'Claggy Mat', you had to wipe your feet on the fucking way out, but most of the pubs around were known more by their nick-name for whatever reason, one being called The Mucky Pots. A few of the lads would take their own glass or tankard with them when they went for a pint there, can't imagine why.

Our area was rife with dog shit, because in those days dogs would be left free to roam the streets, shitting wherever they wanted, but there'd also be owners with their dogs on leads, who must have thought the council had drawn yellow lines in the gutter to show them where there dog could shit without having to pick it up.

Yes being a young lad round our end was always a bit dodgy, you had to dodge just about everything, dog shit, bobbies, the truant officer, teachers, not forgetting me dad, the list was fucking endless...Ah, the bad old days!

3. CLUB DAY TRIP

One of my earliest recollections of mam and dad being together is of a summertime bus trip to Scarborough organised by the Grangetown Unity Club; club outings were among the main highlights of the year, where members saved up with the club on a weekly basis to pay for the treat. If you've ever been to Scarborough, you'll know it's very hilly, Ken Dodd always said after his shows there, that his audience would have to rope themselves together to get back to their digs. Mam was one of five sisters and they had all come along with their husbands, and the oldest sister Ivy, was very loud, in fact she had such a big mouth that dad used to say she probably put her lipstick on with a fucking paint roller.

When we got there, I remember all of us bulldozing into this cafe, it was the first time any of us had seen chairs made from wicker basket weaving, at first I wondered if they were strong enough to sit on because we had some fucking big arses to accommodate. Dad's friend, Les Coats, said, 'they're not very tough, these chairs,' kicked one and, would you believe, broke his ankle. Anyway we all got in and sat down. Now, I'm telling you, if there was a perfume called chip fat then the owner of the cafe could have bottled it and made a fucking fortune, so you can now imagine what the place smelt like. No wonder it was the only place empty enough to take all us lot in one go. The cafe owner employed very small waitresses to make the portions look bigger than they actually were.

Auntie Ivy ordered a salad, and after nearly finishing the meal, she moved a lettuce leaf to find there was a slug on it, well she screamed and everybody turned round, mother said, 'quick, get the health inspector.' Ivy said, 'I could have been killed,' ever so slightly exaggerating. The boss of the cafe came over which resulted in an argument, I thought they were going to start slugging it out there and then...well. There was so much commotion that people out in the street were stopping and looking in to see what was going on, of course during the confrontation it gave everyone else the chance to nick the salt, pepper and vinegar pots, hiding them in their handbags, you could hear them chinking away as we left the cafe.

My sister had been talking to an American woman, about how mushy peas are made, well I'm not sure what the look was on her face, but it was pretty obvious she'd never heard of mushy peas before, 'oh my gawd, son of a bitch, that sounds gross!' she said with a crumpled expression, which was to say the least ironic, considering the shite they shove down their throats over there. She was playing holy hell because she'd asked for a glass of water and had to pay 2d (old money), God only knows what she'd say about the price of water if she was around today.

To some people with us, this bus trip would be their annual holiday, there would be no more excursions until next year and dad would say, 'some people just don't know when they're well off.' Let me tell you that these people certainly weren't well off, in fact most didn't have a penny to scratch their arses with, but they definitely knew how to enjoy themselves when given the opportunity.

On the bus, going home, Les sat next to dad, he said, 'we've had a great day, Colin, apart from my ankle, sun was out, done a bit of shopping, and, of course, we got the meal for next to nothing, thanks to Ivy, turned out to be a stroke of luck her finding that slug just as we'd all finished eating our food.' Dad said, 'Ivy does it all the time, she carries that slug around inside a little pouch in her handbag, then drops it onto her plate when she knows there's nobody looking.' Well I'd never seen dad and Les laugh so much ever.

Dad, second from right with Les and other mates on club trip

4. SPUd

ooking back to the fifties, I was a member of Grangetown Boys' Club and had a nickname of spud, where that came from I don't know. I was never going to be a footballer; but the lads would always say, 'give one-legged spud a game,' one legged because I used to play like I only had one fucking leg. One day, Middlesbrough F. C. came to the club with a machine, a novelty really, because in those days, someone was more likely to turn up with a machine gun than just a machine. The machine measured the speed of a football being kicked into it from a standing position; apparently I won with a kick that was measured at around 50 m.p.h.

This came in handy years later, not because of scraps and fights with other kids but, I was sent to borstal at Portland Bill; they had a football team, and the coaches thought I would make a good goalkeeper. There was a match arranged against Swindon Town Juniors and at half-time it was still 0–0, with me being in goal, I was amazed that the score wasn't fifteen-nil to them, because they were very good; I thought I was going to have to dig a trench around the penalty area to defend my goal. The whole of the borstal turned out to watch the game, and you can imagine the tension, bearing in mind that half of the crowd were rapists, murderers or Liverpudlians. Our team were pretending to be hard knocks; their team were just playing it cool, trying not get injured;

they were probably shitting themselves at having to play a game against a rabble of borstal lads.

Mam, on the left, visited me at Portland Bill

It was very, very windy, so much so that the goalposts were at forty five degrees; it was that windy, when I took a goal-kick, the ball went up in the air being carried by the gale, came down hitting their goalkeeper on the shoulder before bouncing over the goal line and nestling in the back of the net. I was an absolute hero, even though the final score was seven-one, not to us, of course; the gay lags at the borstal were offering me free wanks for weeks. Yes, my goal was the talking point of that borstal for two years, I wouldn't let them forget it, even the screws were nice to me. The next few weeks after my famous goal, were the most exciting times I had in there, because I was actually getting sugar in my tea, and offered extra biscuits, yes, you could stick your free wanks; more biccies for me, please!

5. OUR MAM

Our mam was 71 and lived in a prefab on the Lakes Estate, Redcar, I used to go round three or four times a week, but for mam, that was never enough, I'd often get that phone call saying, 'where are you, I'm still alive you know!' I'd been doing quite well, so I stole her loads of things, like T.V.s, a washing machine, hoover, that sort of stuff, while my luck was still in.

Mam was outspoken to the point of being embarrassing, in fact, while I was round there one day, I was putting the kettle on, when there was a thunderous bang on the front door. I said, 'mam, there's a lady here,' she called back, 'it'll be the home help,' so I opened the door to reveal a very large rotund, authoritative looking lady, what's more, you could have hung a fucking flower basket on her nose. She looked at me and said, 'Mrs Trevethick?' I answered 'well no, actually,' she'd obviously never been in the Observer Corps, 'I'm her son, Royston.' Well I'm not saying she was frightening, but I saw out of the corner of my eye, the budgie throw himself into the cat's mouth; no you certainly wouldn't say anything to annoy a woman like this if you didn't want a knuckle sandwich. Mam's dog growled, bad mistake, then come to his senses and quickly ran under the settee, these pets had obviously met her before, her face was more frightening than the illustrations in Hannibal Lecter's cook book.

Sounding a bit like Paul Robeson, who was a black gospel singer with a very deep baritone voice back in the fifties, she said, 'I've come to bath your mother.' Mam looked her straight in the crutch and said, 'you're not one of those lesbians are you?' She said, 'no, dear, I do have a husband and four kids.' I wanted to say to my mother, 'you know, some men like bad breath, lots of spots, and a nose like a blind cobbler's thumb,' but didn't have the bottle, she would have probably knocked me into the middle of the next fucking week. Mam said rather loudly, 'be careful with my back,' the home help replied, 'yes, Mrs Trevethick, why fake a day's illness when you can make it last a whole week?' I could feel a fight coming on, so I made a quick exit out of the door.

Mam never was a great cook, and there wasn't much money around when we were kids, so at meal times, if any of us lads ever dared to ask for an extra slice of gravy, there'd be fucking hell on. I do remember one occasion though, it was a Sunday morning, when mam came to me in a quiet corner and told me we had a guest coming for Sunday dinner. This was unheard of in those days. Well, my mam wanted to make an impression, so she said to me, 'I've made a rabbit pie but it's not very big, so when I ask who wants a piece of rabbit pie, I need you to say 'none for me thanks mam,' because I want to make sure there's enough to go round, have you got that, son?' I said, 'that's ok, mam', not feeling too bothered really, because mam's rabbit pie had never been anything to write home about; do you know, she always used to look for a rabbit with a humpty back so it would help keep the pie crust up.

Anyway, our guest arrived and everything was going to plan, mam asked, 'who wants rabbit pie?' and I played along and said, 'none for me thanks, mam.' Everybody tucked in and ate their meal, I nearly said enjoyed, but that would have been taking it too far, then after dinner, this great big bowl of trifle came out. I thought, 'fuck me, I can't remember the last time we had trifle,' and mam hadn't mentioned it at all, so when she asked, 'who wants trifle?' with a big smile on my face, I chirped up saying, 'I'll have some trifle, mam,' there was a moments silence, then she came back using my Sunday name, 'you will not, our Royston,' continuing quite loudly, 'you wouldn't eat your rabbit pie!' I thought, 'fucking hell!'

Because The Lakes Estate was quite rough, on bonfire night there was at least six fireworks pushed through our letter box, so many that our brand new welcome mat got burned beyond recognition. I spotted one fat lad trying to run away and gave chase, when I caught up with him he was totally out of breath, so I gave him a fucking good kick up the arse just for good measure. Within half an hour his father came round to the house shouting his mouth off at me, but mam was stood right behind me inside the door, and I'll never forget her penetrating words as long as I live, 'hey, mate, next time you let that lad of yours out of the house, dress him up as a penis, because he's a little fat fucking prick,'... yes, on the Lakes Estate you had give as good as you got!

6. The Lakes (But not as you know them)

When I lived on the Lakes Estate, at 9 Norfolk Close, which was just around the corner from my mother's house, next door to us lived a couple in their forties, John and Jean; they met at the backward school, so, you can gather, they weren't a full shilling. She wasn't so stupid though, she'd go into town, do her shopping, pretend to faint, and get a lift home in an ambulance, Jean wasn't so fucking daft after all. They bought a dog, and, because they liked me, they called it Roy, so you can imagine when they called the dog in, shouting in the garden, Roy, Roy, I kept coming out of our house saying, 'John, what do you want?' I had to have a word and said, 'John for fuck's sake, will you change that dog's name?' He changed it to Chubby (not really).

I never ever saw John and Jean look smart, in fact if they'd stolen clothes from a scarecrow they would have looked better, but I always felt a bit sorry for them so I gave them an old dining room carpet I was going to throw out. They'd had the carpet for about two days when there was a knock on my door at about one o'clock in the morning, 'I thought I'd better tell you that the dog's shit on your carpet, Roy,' I said, 'John, it's not my carpet anymore, I gave it to you, it's your job to clean it up, and while you're here, will you stop the dog barking day and night?' He said, 'yes, I'm sorry about that, but, you see, he's always pleased to see us when we come home,' gormless fucker, 'and another thing, Roy, he's trying to mate with Jean's leg,' I said, 'in that case, you want to take him to fucking Specsaver's, 'cos there's something wrong with his eyesight, or, at least, tell Jean to shave her fucking legs,' and then I, ever so politely, shut the door on him and went back to bed.

7. Mags, Bags and Dirty Slags

When it came to magazines 'Penthouse' was regarded as far too expensive, so I used to buy a mag called 'Spick and Span', where you didn't see any fannies just tits, though that was quite a turn on in those days. You see I was still a young man hoping to become sexually active but, having been blessed with a fat face and a fat belly, if I was lucky enough to have a sexual encounter I was usually on my own, well me and 'Spic and Span'. There was no such thing as aids, we hadn't been told about condoms, and anal sex was just something your dog used to do, so to be honest our sex lives were as boring as fuck; or was that just me?

Have you noticed when you're out with a mate, if you see a good looker, she usually has an ugly friend tagging along, which was always dead lucky for me or I would never have got fixed up. You see I'd be the one taking home the little fat ugly fucker, yes we'd be attracted to each other like fucking magnets. Why do you think?...well listen, I couldn't even get a pole dancer to take any money off me, or get fixed up in a brothel with twenty pound notes sticking out of my fucking ears, but still, a fuck's a fuck, you can always bash away and think of someone else. A pal once said, 'Roy, while you're shagging you should have some music playing in the background, but be careful what you play because if it's a song you know you just might start singing along, or maybe humming if you've got a face full of hairy pie; you ought to try it, sounds a bit like playing a comb and paper, but with a great echo! In those days, I was really fast when it came to making love and got far too excited, far too quickly, it was always over in a flash, could have been the music I was playing though, you see my favourite piece of music at the time was '*The flight of the bumble bee*'. You just try shagging in time to '*The flight of the bumble bee*' and see what happens, I was that fucked afterwards I had to go and see a chiropractor; well I think that's what you call them, I think he has a chiro and he practises it.

I was told don't be too clever with women either, by saying things like, 'oh, I'm rather large down there,' only for her to find out you were talking about your fucking feet. When I was fourteen and naive, a girl said to me one night, 'would you like me to suck it?' I stupidly said, 'no it's all right thanks, I've got a plaster on it now, look,' thinking she was talking about my thumb which I'd cut with a knife.

I once read that all men were potential rapists, but I think if everyone walked around naked, I'm sure there wouldn't be any rapes, because men would say, 'woh! I'm not going with that, she's got tits like slate layers' nail-bags and her arse droops further than a orang-utan's arms, and what's more she's got a tattoo on her cock!'

When I read those live letters people send in to the likes of Dear Deidre, I crack up at some of the stories, like the other day someone had written, 'dear Heartfelt, my name is Tracy and my boyfriend comes home every night expecting me just to be lying on the bed with my legs open, even before he's had his tea.' She received an answer from someone who said, 'dear Heartfelt, what a lucky bastard you are Tracy, I always have to wait until after tea to be shagged,' signed fat Sarah.

Even at my age now, I still wonder why Prawn crisps taste like women's piss, but I'm not telling you how I know. I have a theory that women love sex right up until their bodies start to sag. Not that it really bothers me that much because for ten years I just went out with my wrist; well you don't have to take it for a meal, or drop it off home after a night out so you save on petrol, it never asks for money, best of all is you don't have to walk round the fucking clothes shops with it, and finally, it never gets a fucking headache.

I think women are bit like shopping trolleys, fascinating and you can't really do without them, but every now and then you get a real awkward one that wants to lead you straight up the fucking aisle, passed the frozen peas.

I'd heard that you can laugh a girl straight into bed, so one night when I took a new girl home I thought I'd do something rather amusing. When we were back at my house, I thought I'd sneak upstairs and put my sister's frock and wig on, then come down and say 'hello', in a sisterly voice. But what happened was, while I was upstairs changing, she was sat waiting for me downstairs, when she must have thought to herself I need a piss, dead classy like. So she came upstairs, looking for the toilet, opened the bedroom door by mistake, and saw me standing there in a black dress with a ginger wig on, well before I could explain, she just blurted out, 'what the fuck?' not so classy like. Well, it was just like the scene from Psycho where Norman Bates dressed up as his dead mother, then on top of that, she glanced out of the bedroom window, and shrieked, 'there's another fucking clown coming up

your garden path, wearing a big red nose, floppy trousers and san-
dals.' I said, 'who do you think you're slagging off, that's my dad
coming home from the pub, and by the way that's his best clobber.'
She replied, 'come to think of it, I can see the fucking resemblance
now,' then grabbed her bag and fucked off out of the front door
as fast as she could. Dad walked in to find me still dressed in my
sister's clobber, well he must have had a good night at the pub,
because he looked straight at me saying, 'goodnight Barbara,' as he
passed, then went straight up the stairs to bed.

8. YER FUCKING JOKING AREN'T YER?

Some of the gags I got away with in the sixties
(By the skin if my teeth)

Wife went to the doctor's. When she came back she was telling me about it. I said, 'did he mention your big fat arse.' She said, 'no, we didn't talk about you at all.'

A policeman caught two queers having sex in a back alley, so he chased after them and they ran off. He knew they must be around somewhere, so he shouted, 'Aye, you need hide; if I catch up with either of you, I'm going to shove this truncheon right up your arse.' A voice came back, 'I'm in the bin.'

Went to the doctor's, I said, 'I've got an awful tummy ache.' Doctor said, 'what do you eat, during an average day?' I said, 'well, for breakfast I'll have, three bowls of cornflakes, bacon, sausage, tomatoes, baked beans, black pudding, fried egg, three slices of fried bread, washed down with four cups of tea. Then about ten o'clock the tea lady comes round at work and I have four slices of cheese on toast, two Kit-Kats and two cups of coffee. At lunch time our meals are subsidised, so I have a three course meal, with starter of soup, prawn cocktail, for main, usually, roast beef and Yorkshire puddings, finishing off with two helpings of treacle sponge and custard. Mid afternoon, I try not to eat too much; I'll have a few Snickers Bars a packet of digestive biscuits and a cup of coffee. Then for my main meal on a night, I'll normally call for a take away, get myself a set meal for two, after I've been the pub for half a dozen pints.' The doctor said, 'drop your trousers, Roy, and bend over.' He took a close look at me from behind, then said, 'I can see what the problem is, Roy, you've only got one fucking arsehole!'

After a booking the other night, I was carried out of the club shoulder high. I said, 'you're ok lads, I can walk to the bus.' They said, 'bus? You're going in the fucking river!'

I told my wife I liked black underwear, so she didn't wash my vest for a month.

Been a busy week, sold our house, the council's going mad.

Doctor, people think I'm a liar. You don't expect me to believe that do you?

Stood at the bar and a fellow said, 'I'm sixty two today,' I said, 'that's good, let me buy you a drink, will you be in tomorrow, he said, 'no I'm on two to ten tomorrow.'

We call our dog Sambuca, because he's a good licker.

Getting married is a bit like sitting on a toilet seat, it feels good but you don't know who's been there before you.

At Christmas, our lass said, 'darling, are you going to kiss me under the mistletoe?' I said, 'I wouldn't even kiss you under chloroform.'

He had an orphan's breakfast, snap, crackle, but no pop.

She lifted her skirt up and pulled her knickers down, her fanny looked like a bite out of a doughnut.

The missus said, 'should I go to the fancy dress party as Long John Silver?' I said, 'no pet, because your parrot stinks.'

She thought a Zulu was a toilet at Longleat Safari Park.

Wife's having stomach trouble at the moment, she can't pull her knickers over it.

Sat in the car with a girl, she said, 'would you like to see where I had my operation,' I said, 'would I!' she said, 'that's the hospital over there.'

'Hi George, I haven't seen you for two years, what have you been doing?' George said, 'two years.'

9. Big Night Out in Redcar

I used to drink in a local pub, The Clarendon in Redcar, one particular night there were only two spare seats near the juke box with two big girls sat at the same table. We were drinking Newcastle Brown Ale, which was our tipple in those days, and we struck up an intelligent conversation with one of the girls, who said, 'I've never heard of Newcastle Brown Ale before,' must have come from fucking Mars, and I don't think she'd never heard of a skipping rope either, looking at the bastard size of her. She said, 'where are you going when you leave here?' I replied, 'we always go to the Starlight Club, it's open 'till two. 'Is it ok if we come along?' 'Be my guest pet, it's a free country,' then looked at her up and down thinking, you're such a fucking big lass, you might have to pay for two people at the door.

We were stood in a queue, which was quite long, while other girls were walking in at the front. One of the girls who'd come along with us shouted out, 'get to the back of the queue, you slags,' which started an argument. Then these lads joined in, 'get to the back of the queue, what do you think we're stood here for, the good of our fucking health?' By this time, we'd budged up towards the door as scuffles broke out with people pushing and shoving. Somebody must have said something to the doorman, which incidentally wasn't me, but he turned round to punch me and he hit this girl full belt in the face sending her to the floor like a sack of spuds. When I looked at him I could see who it was, it was Sean, now I know Sean's cock-eyed so he obviously meant to hit me, but belted this girl instead, which I'm sure he wished he hadn't because by the time I could draw a breath, she'd leapt up and flattened him, knocking him for six. After the melee had calmed down, I looked down at the pavement to see there were two gold chain necklaces laid next to a watch, so I bent down and put them straight in my pocket. My shirt was ripped, I got a black eye, spewed up, lost my wallet, but got a wank on the beach; what a fucking great night out, and then on top of that I got twenty quid from the pawnshop for the stuff I picked up off the floor!

10. FLat BROKe

Years ago, I shared a rented flat in Saltburn-by-the-Sea; now if you knew Saltburn, you'd be aware that it's so dull the corner shop sells postcards of another town. A friend asked me why I moved from Redcar and I said, 'I didn't want to move, I was dragged screaming by my new flat-mates.' So there we were, four of us renting this flat which was a shithole, and there were mice, but I don't think they'd had a good feed since the last tenants had left, still you know what it's like when you're sharing a flat, you did have your exciting times.

There's a saying that two heads are better than one, I said, 'yes, but not if they're on the same neck.' We were trying to keep our heads above water, which is not easy when you live so close to the sea, but my dad always said that it should be easy for us, because wood floats. Mam said, 'your dad's a bit of a wit,' I said, 'well, you're half right,' (half-wit).

We used to argue in the flat over things like who owned the last tea bag in the box, and whoever won the argument got first use of the tea bag, then it would be handed to the next one and so on, until ultimately, the fourth cup of tea was made up of plain hot water, you still weren't guaranteed of it tasting anything like unless you'd won the fight over the last of the sugar and milk. The landlord, we called him 'grim death', would come on a Friday to collect forty pounds which was a tenner each, we knew his knock on the door, it was 'bang, bang, bang, come on I know you're in there!' Then he'd shout, 'rent!' and we'd shout, 'spent!'

Bang, bang, bang,
I know you're in there!

To make the electric fire work we had to feed it ten pence pieces, so we'd cut the lino up into the shape of ten pence pieces and used them, but at the end of the month, when the landlord came along to empty the fire, he said that we had to have the floor re-laid at our expense.

In case any of us got fixed up and took a girl back we had a secret knock on the door, it was the same one we all used:- dat-da-da-dah-da---da-da, or something like that. One night, I was taking a girl to the bus stop to go home when we found out her bus had already gone, this was before we had mobile phones, so we had to find a telephone box for her to ring her mam. She said to her mam, 'I'm staying with my friend Jackie, I'll be alright, see you in the morning.' Back at the flat, one thing lead to another, and then the secret knock came on the door, dat-da-da-dah-da—dada, I said to her, 'ssshhhh, don't say a word,' but then dat-da-da-dah—da-da came again. Finally I shouted, 'I'm just having my supper,' one of the lads said, 'we've been to the pub and brought fish and chips back for you, so hurry up and finish your supper, mucky cunt!'

JUST HAVING A BIT OF SUPPER ?

11. Hard Times

got crabs when I was sixteen, but how do you think I knew? well not because my penis started walking sideways I can tell you. So I had to go to the doctors', and how embarrassing do you think that was? It could have been worse though, he could have told me I was pregnant.

A few years after that, there I was, married with two children, and I needed a steady job with a steady income, so I took a job on a construction site mixing darbo for plasterers, but I was being treated like shit, and hated the job. I used to go to work real tired, then once the gaffer caught me on a bad day, when he gave me a load of grief over something and nothing. So I whacked him with the only thing I had to hand, a full bucket of cement, the poor bucket didn't know what hit it. After appearing at the magistrates' court, where I was charged with the illegal use of a bucket full of cement, I was fined two hundred pounds. I was sure it wouldn't get that far, because I didn't really think they had anything concrete to go on, and thankfully it didn't turn me into a hardened criminal, but as a punishment I had to see a Probation Officer once every two weeks.

I was at such a low ebb at that time, with arguments at home, yes I remember lying in bed with the wife one night; I was lying to her and she was lying to me. It was probably one of the least creative periods of my life and I was becoming so frustrated, but I'd taught myself to play the drums, securing a little job at the Station Hotel in Redcar, where I was introduced to the demon drink, but it was a welcome escape from the realities of everyday life, because it was great fun and we were laughing all the time.

In those days, people were continuously worrying about their insecurity, many had just experienced the post war years, but times were now in a period of change; it was the sixties, and the young crowd which was us lot, were going to rule the world and live forever. It was the time of mini-skirts and hot-pants, girls' legs appeared to go up as far as the eye could see and then a bit further, all of us lads were walking around with a constant fucking hard on. We used all the sixties' jargon back then like, 'lay it on me', 'baby' or 'cool', nowadays everyone just gets called 'bro', or something similar. When it came to slang back then, we didn't mince our words, we just said it as it was, 'why don't you just go and fuck yourself?'

I could always find something to do, in fact I had a great line in the selling on of second hand goods for a living, nudge, nudge, wink, wink, ask no questions, know what I mean? But it wasn't really what I would have called a living, more like a scrap for survival, and I was constantly on the lookout for other ventures.

Even now, looking back over the years of doing stand-up, I can see that I was always writing little lines down about everyday occurrences, then trying them out on people, you see trying to be funny simply can't be turned on and off at will. I was getting laughs and got hooked, so I would go anywhere like the Fairway pub in Dormanstown. Now I got real cocky when I went there, I took to the microphone and had the audience in the palm of my hand, they were laughing like fuck, I must say I was feeling rather pleased with myself, until I got told that most of the audience had been in since the pub opened and were pissed off their faces. Still I was thinking to myself, I've got something special here, but believe me, it certainly doesn't work out just like that, because in this business, one minute you can be on top of the world, then you can soon be brought back down to earth with one fucking big bang!

12. MY Old flat

The flat I had in Redcar was above Beryl's hairdressing shop, it stunk of perms, except on Tuesdays when the shop offered a discount for the O.A.P. blue rinse brigade, on those days all you could smell was dried piss. The rest of the week, the stench of perm solution in the air was so strong that you could actually taste it. If you made a sandwich the crusts would curl up all by themselves, and if I stayed in the flat too long, my lips would also start to curl as though I was doing an impression of Mick fucking Jagger!

It was at that time that I bought my first piano, £5.00 from Walker's Salerooms, fucking bargain, although I don't think the man in the flat next door would have agreed. He died soon afterwards and I think my piano playing must have killed him off, besides the fact that he smoked a hundred fags a day, that is. In my flat I had a rickety old bed that had more cracks in it than Jimmy Cricket and Tim Vine's acts put together. I popped to the shop one morning, which was about six hundred yards away, and on returning I discovered a stranger standing in the middle of my living room. I said, 'can I help you, mate?' he said, 'oh, I'm sorry, I must have walked into the wrong flat,' and, like a fucking idiot, I let him walk out. It wasn't 'till he'd gone I realised some of my stuff was missing, but I should have twigged what he was up to really, people don't normally walk round wearing a balaclava in the middle of a fucking heatwave do they?

My pride and joy was a Dansette record player with a five watt speaker, you would have had to put your head under the lid to experience surround sound, but I thought it was marvellous. At the time it was regarded as 'straight out of the arc technology!' The rent for my flat was £10.00 per week, so it always left me with enough money to buy a few records, and there was a second-hand shop just around the corner that had loads of old records, which they sold dirt cheap; I remember buying some of them, like Tony Joe White and Santana.

This was also when I started getting a few stand up jobs, the beginning of my career if you like, I'd usually get around fifteen quid for doing a one hour spot. I was also doodling little lines down about things that had I'd seen while I'd been out, and it was then I realised that when you go shopping, just look around, there's something funny happening all of the time, you just have to pick up on it. The flat wasn't perfect, the floor was sticky around the piss pot, I can't imagine why, and so were the sheets, but that's a different story. I've never been much of a handy-man, but a knob came off the electric cooker, so I thought it would be a good idea to stick a fork in the hole where the knob had been. Well fuck me, if my dog could have talked, I'm sure he'd have said, 'Roy just flew passed me doing forty miles an hour,' because I hit the wall on the other side of the kitchen with such force that my cap fell off and the electric shock had turned my hair into a fucking crew-cut, with my eyebrows smoking away like they'd been blow torched. What a silly fucker, but I suppose you'd expect that from somebody who burns salad.

13. FIRSTS

The first club I ever played, I got twenty-five quid for three one hour spots, it was the type of club people would go to just to throw themselves off the fucking roof. I was on with self-named 'Billy the Hero'; he was a hero because when his dad was killed in a miner's accident, Billy was the one who managed to find the hidden insurance policy. Apparently, Billy had won a karaoke competition at his local pub aptly named 'The Fiddlers', because they were all on benefits, but It was rumoured that he only won the competition because most of his family were the judges.

Billy, was a funny looking lad with a glass eye, wooden leg and a hump on his back which he swore had been following him about all day, he was a bugger for giving the girls the eye, then politely asking for it back, before he went home, always asking if he could see them again, his little joke. He did a song with a one string ukulele, now correct me if I'm wrong, but I'm sure a ukulele would normally have four strings, though I'm not always right. In fact I actually thought Ringo Starr was a drummer, mind you Billy could have shown Ringo a thing or two, keeping time with his one string ukulele by tapping along with his wooden leg. Billy's opening song was '*Goodbye Cruel World*', but to be honest the world hadn't seemed that fucking cruel until Billy started singing. If I'd had my way he'd have said goodbye to the cruel world at least four fucking years earlier.

We had a similar competition at our local pub, but it's in a very rough area, and the winner of our competition got a hamper full of amphetamines, in fact there were so many drugs in the hamper that it attracted more than two thousand entrants. I would have come third, but I'd just been in the gents' toilet, where it was hard to breathe because of the smell of piss and shit, that when I tried to sing nothing came out, I couldn't even catch my fucking breath. It was in that toilet that I saw my first bit of graffiti, which had been written above the piss-pot and I had to laugh because it said, 'Christine, if you are reading this, then we're finished', and on the back of the toilet door it said, 'after you have emptied your arse, please ask the barmaid for a toilet roll,' a bit fucking late for that I thought.

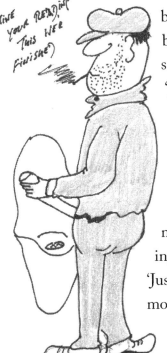

That same night, I thought I'd been recognised because of my show business career, when this bloke said, 'I know you, don't I?' I said, 'you could do,' thinking he must be referring to me being a comedian, he said, 'yes I do, you stood on my fucking foot in Asda last week,'...I thought fucking hell fame at last.

At my first official engagements, there were other acts appearing, I was billed on the posters as 'Just Support', so when I went for my money that night, he said, 'who are you?' I said, 'just Support.' Then by the time the Concert Chairman put me on that night, the cleaners were waiting to come in, and if the barmaids hadn't stopped back, I'd have had nobody to perform to. Part of my contract was to help empty the ashtrays and sweep the floor before I went home. The only thing I got a round of applause for, but they could fuck off if they thought I was going to do a encore, I wasn't cleaning the fucking bogs out for them; you know, I'd heard acts saying after a gig that they'd cleaned up, but until then I really didn't know what they meant.

Afterwards I rang up a comic friend of mine and said, 'you won't believe this, my first proper gig and I've just died a death,' he said, 'I hope you asked them for funeral expenses?'

14. Band Days

They never asked me to sing in my first band, it was pretty obvious why, probably because they weren't as deaf as a fucking door post, but I can still see myself, as a boy, stood in front of the mirror singing into a hair brush, thinking I was Elvis Presley. I'm sure the only reason I thought I was really good then, was because I didn't have to audition just to stand in front of my mirror.

One night, whilst working in the Four Man Band, we had a local gig in the North East, and I'd brought an old girlfriend along with me; that's someone I used to go out with not an old age pensioner I'd picked up on the way, just in case you were thinking. I was driving the van that night and as we turned a corner in Grangetown, Sunderland, there was a car parked in a real awkward spot which I nearly hit, but luckily managed to swerve and miss by a midge's. Usually this would have resulted in a tirade of verbal abuse directed at the empty vehicle but, because I was on my best behaviour having got a special passenger in the car, i.e. my old girlfriend, I stifled what I really wanted to say, and blurted out, 'that's a silly place to park!' Well, the lads looked at each other, and then altogether turned to look at me, then as one, burst into the most uncontrollable laughing fit I've ever seen. From that day on, if anyone brought a girl along to a gig, whoever's girlfriend it was, would always say to the rest of the lads, 'don't forget, 'it's a silly place to park night, tonight.'

Right from the early comedy group days, we always prided ourselves with doing unique, original material, but this wasn't always what people wanted. One night, working in the Four Man Band, we had a booking at a geordie pit village club, and during the break I was relieving myself in the gents when a club member, looking very serious said, 'enjoyed your show bonny lad, but can't you tell us a joke we know?' Some people just need to know when they have to laugh. I bumped into him not much later in the night, when he was standing at the bar, I say standing, but it was not so much standing, more like wobbling about the same as a fucking Hartley's jelly that hadn't quite set right. He'd just put his hand in his pocket, pulled out a small wad of cash, and looked the barmaid straight in the eye saying, 'waye, ya bugger a hell,' (A polite Geordie expression of disbelief), 'I've just got enough left for fourteen pints, hinny.'

♫ 15. Oh we do like to be beside the sea-side ♫

'm guessing you've probably seen the pictures before of Dec Vasey's Four Man Band with the piano on Redcar beach; they've been in previous publications but, by now, they probably deserve some sort of explanation. The Four Man Band progressed from our earlier band, The Pipeline, becoming more of a comedy show-group. We had already played a few venues, and were starting to make a name for ourselves, so it was decided we should have some publicity photos. At the time I lived in Redcar East, just a stone's throw from the beach, you could tell which house was ours, all the bastard windows were broke.

There was a piano in the living room, and, as you would do, in those days, early 70s, I decided to wallpaper it, this was, of course, before I seriously took up playing the piano. What I used as wallpaper were publicity posters that had been used to advertise our appearances on various social clubs in the North East. Each agency that you worked for had their own posters, which they sent to clubs advertising forthcoming acts with the date they were due to appear, they were normally drawn up by the agents them-selves, or someone else in the office. The posters would carry crazy superlatives to describe the acts, such as 'Voice of the Century' or 'Man in the White Suite', three piece with a nice comfy settee, apparently. On a personal level they often got our name wrong; instead of Dec Vasey, they would write Peck Frazer, Dick Varsey or some other stupid name.

Back to the piano, it was decided that a good publicity stunt would be to launch the piano from the beach, and have the occa-sion photographed for prosperity. In those days, doing something like that never occurred to us as being a bit strange, we never really thought about the consequences of our actions then. I got in touch with a local photographer, Derek Richardson, and he agreed to meet us on the beach at an arranged time, to take some photographs, but I'm not really sure he knew what he was letting himself in for.

On the day in question we loaded the piano into the van, not an easy task, as you can imagine, those old upright pianos are as heavy as fuck. There was only me with any meat on my bones, the rest of the lads were as thin as rakes, so you can tell what kind of a performance we had just getting this piano off the floor, never mind into the back of the fucking van, ah...dedication. Our Dec was really thin, I used to tell a crack on stage about him going to the swimming baths, diving in, and the attendant shouting, 'who threw them braces in there?' So, with the piano in the back of the van, surprised we didn't break the suspension, probably didn't have any, off we went to the beach, which was only a matter of a few hundred yards away.

Once there we met up with Mr Richardson, the photographer, and drove the van down the slip-way used by the local fishermen. We'd chosen a section of the beach which was well away from any day trippers that could have been around, thankfully the tide was not too far out, and on its way back in. We had the same palaver getting the piano out, as we did getting it in, so we had to make sure we got it out exactly where we wanted it, because there would be no budging it once it had settled itself in the sand. We positioned the piano near the water's edge, so the waves could lap up against it, eventually getting it in a position that we were happy with. Now it was time for us to change into our new stage clothes; we'd managed to find something suitably ridiculous from several local second hand shops.

So there we were, Dec, Lee, George and I, undressing in the middle of Redcar beach, by this time Mr Richardson the photographer, must have been wondering what on Earth was going on, and should he make a run for it now, or what? He didn't get the chance, we were soon changed and ready to assume poses, around the piano, and like a true professional, Mr Richardson threw himself into his job head first, quite literally really, because he was hit by the first strong wave and went arse over tit into the briny, we were ok because we had a piano to hang on to. A trooper to the end, Mr Richardson carried on even though soaked to the skin, because thankfully, he was able to save his camera equipment from getting wet. We've all been in similar positions when carrying a drink, if we slip over whilst carrying a pint we always manage to save our beer without spilling a drop, don't we?

As you can see from the photograph, we got the job done, but by this time, the tide was coming in quite fast, and as we had finished the sea water was now lashing up against the sides of the piano. I don't think we had thought as far as what we were going to do with the piano afterwards, but that was answered for us by the next wave. The piano was already becoming unsteady and suddenly it fell backwards, quite slowly, landing flat on its back, reminiscent of the final moments of the Titanic, and It gave out a quite sad, muffled chord; ♪ b flat with an augmented seventh, if my memory serves me well, as it met its final resting place, on the sea bed. We decided to have one last photograph taken, and then with the waves still lashing over the now, prostrate instrument, we had no choice but to leave it to its watery grave and return to the van before we were cut off by the incoming tide. Once back in the van we beat a hasty retreat and got ourselves changed out of our wet stage clothes.

The next morning, I was woken quite early by loud knocking on my front door. It was a Policeman who obviously didn't have a fucking sense of humour at all, because when he said, 'do you know you've left your piano on the beach?' I said, 'no, but I do know ♫ I've left my heart in San Francisco ♫, but I can't play it for you right now because someone broke into my house last night, while I was at work, and stole my piano.' The miserable twat just said, 'likely story, the Coast-Guard told me he saw some rather strange looking individuals yesterday, messing about on the beach with a piano.' 'Can't have been me, Officer,' I said, 'I've just finished doing a double at I.C.I.' Still, not believing a word of it, he reluctantly left saying, 'you haven't heard the last of this.'

Anyway, he never came back, the piano stayed put and must have sank into the sea-bed, it will still be there now 45 years on, but I'm sure everything will have rotted away by now, apart from the black and white ivory keys. I imagine if Tony Robinson and his time machine came along and uncovered it during an archaeological dig, he'll probably think he's discovered a sea monster from the Neolithic ages that died with a fucking big smile on its face; I know, we all still smile about it.

16. Heavy Night and a Packet of Crisps

Dek Vasey's Four Man Band was, as you may already know, a comedy show band; the first set was comedy routines from start to finish, interspersed with popular commercial songs from the charts, then the second set was for dancing. Everything was aimed at entertaining the regular workingmen's club audience, but this still didn't stop dickhead agents sending us, on a Friday night, to any one of the pit village clubs to perform at their heavy-metal nights. In fact the agent who'd sent us to one in particular, I'm sure, wanted fucking tazing. This place was just a deafening hell hole and I think we were to be the nights sacrifice at the altar, I'm almost certain they had pig's blood on draught. The club was such a shit hole that you could have improved it by spreading horse manure on the fucking dance floor, and putting a pig in the bar as an air freshener.

One bloke spewed up during our opening number, so I shouted to him, 'what's the matter mate, don't you like '*Octopus's Garden?*' I had to tell the lads that a committee man had asked us not to smile on stage, because if we did we'd be creating too much excitement for the youngsters that were in. Not much chance of us smiling here anyway, well not until we got the fuck out and were on our way home. Also, he'd asked us to try and only buy one drink or the club members would think the committee were all on the fiddle and were giving us a backhander, although how we were going to get through this one with only one drink was going to be some task.

As I said earlier, it was usually a Friday night in these clubs which was dedicated to a much younger audience, who would come along to hear some heavy metal, Led Zeppelin, Black Sabbath, Deep Purple, Free, you get the idea. These kids wanted music, sorry a sound that they could shake their heads to until their eardrums burst and blood poured from every available orifice. So when we came on stage, dressed like some refugees from the 1920s and opened up with The Beatles 'Octopus's Garden', you can imagine the look of horror on their faces. There'd always be some stupid cunt that would come to the front of the stage and shout up, 'do you know "Smoke on the Water"?' The reply would always be the same; 'are you fucking blind as well as deaf, look at what we're wearing, listen to what we're playing, do we look like we're going to play 'Smoke on the fucking Water', you brainless fucking twat.' None of which he would have heard, because although we were playing 'Octopus's Garden', it was quite a bit louder than it usually, still trying in vain to satisfy the natives, you see. All the same, if we had been able to make anyone's ears bleed with our version of 'Octopus's Garden', no matter how loud, we would probably have ended up in the Guinness Book of Records.

As usual, at these gigs, by the end of the first set, there was a line of committee men queuing up to tell us how shit we were, that we were being paid off, and would never appear on their club ever again...ah, every cloud, as they say. It had happened to us so many times, it dawned on me that these Friday night clubs probably only ever paid for one spot and fucked every band off at half time, whether they played 'Smoke on the fucking Water' or not.

It was after one these nights, paid off at half time, that I said to the lads, 'get the gear in the van, I won't be long,' then disappeared out of the club, so the lads dismantled everything, got the van loaded up, and waited for me to come back. When I got back, I jumped into the passenger seat and said, 'get your foot down,' one of the lads said, 'why, where have you been?' I said, 'I've been to the local Police Station and told them there are underage people in the club, drinking alcohol, playing bingo, and eating crisps,' someone said, 'eating crisps? We'd better fuck off quick, before the S.W.A.T. team arrives.'

17. van Dam (Damn van)

One of the vans we had in the early days was a Bedford some-thing or another and, considering the condition of it, we would have been wise to make it look inconspicuous, but no, nothing like that would ever dawn on us in those days, this was the band's van and we wanted to be noticed. The fact that it had four baldy tyres, no wing mirrors, body work hanging off and a very annoyingly loud exhaust would have been enough to get us to stand out from anything else on the road, but we needed more. I arranged to have the van painted lime green, so they'd definitely see us coming now, but I still didn't think it was noticeable enough and wanted to make a statement, so as It was around the time of 'flower power', back end of the sixties going into the seventies, I got someone to paint large flowers on the both sides of it. Looked absolutely great, not only was it the best looking band van in the area, but I thought it would be the perfect shagging wagging, tell me what red blooded female would give up the opportunity of a lift in a van ordained with her favourite flowers? None is the word you're looking for, if I ever got fixed up, which was usually with the fat ugly bird left behind by her mates, one look at the transport home and you could physically see them pulling their knickers up until they were round their necks, at the same time as frantically searching their pockets for some spare cash to get a taxi home. In fact one fat lass took one look at the van and said she would rather go home in a fucking hearse. I said, 'that can be arranged,' cheeky, fat, fucking bastard split-arse!

Well, the van, as I said before, was essentially for the band to get to and from gigs. Each of us would be picked up from home on the way, I remember calling a bit early for Dec one night, only to find him in the kitchen of his flat, holding an egg on a spoon under the hot water tap, I said, 'Dec, what are you doing,' he said, 'I'm trying to boil an egg for my tea,' no we weren't a domesticated lot. I remember being stopped by the Police one night, on my way to pick the lads up. A Policeman got out of his car and came over to me and said, 'you were breaking the speed limit, you were doing fifty miles an hour.' I said, 'I can't have been officer, I've only been out twenty minutes.' Bum, Bum.

The flowery Bedford, as I said before wasn't in great shape, in fact I'd call it a typical band wagon of its day, we'd pass or meet other bands at service stations and most of their vans were in the same nick as ours, but having said that it was as though these vehicles knew they had a job to do, and by hook or by crook they would always get us to the venue.

There was one night in particular, we'd all been picked up and some of the band had invited their girlfriends along, we were going to a club in Newcastle, and we were all packed into the van along with our equipment, or gear as it was known. There were no proper back seats in the van so P. A. speakers and other stuff were arranged to create a seating area for whoever had to sit there. Then off we would go, there was no sat-nav in those days, so the agent would give us the name of the club and the town or village it was in, not even a street name usually, then when we got there late, the Concert Chairman would usually complain like fuck because we couldn't find the club in time and had to carry our gear in while the bingo flyer was on, fucking sacrilege.

When we went to Newcastle the A19 was always the favoured route, and there's a small village just north of Billingham called Sheraton. At this point, on the A19, there is the most gentlest of inclines you would ever experience in motoring, I can only liken it to the slope from Twiggy's chest to her nipple; practically none existent. Well our van used to struggle like fuck to negotiate this 'mountainous climb' so much that we used to call this part of the journey 'Sheraton Bank'.

On this night on our way to the booking, whilst groaning up 'Sheraton Bank', someone in the back noticed a smell of burning, so we immediately pulled over and all jumped out; sure enough, there were flames coming from under the back of the van, not too far away from the petrol tank. We were all thinking how the fuck were we going to put this out? It was never heard of, in those days, to carry a fire extinguisher, and there was no supply of water about, so it didn't take us too long to realise the only way this fire was going to go out was if somebody were to piss on it. We had three girls in the van and, it was pretty obvious that with no directional sense to their slash, they were going be of no fucking use at all, so it was down to us lads. The girls were sent off behind some bushes to protect our modesty, although I'm pretty sure there would have been a bit of peeping and girlie giggling going on.

I was the first to try, so I got my hose out and pointed it towards the flames, but to no avail, I really didn't want a slash, and try as I might, nothing was happening. The incident was quickly turning into something of an episode from a *Carry On* film, so when Davy took out his dick, he couldn't point it in the right direction for laughing. 'You'll have to put it out, George,' I shouted. 'But, I don't want one,' came the reply, 'you'll just have to have a go, or the whole fucking van's going to go up in flames, taking our fucking gear with it.' Well, insisting that he really didn't want to go, yet still doing a great impression of Fireman Sam by directing his appendage towards the flames, opening the stop cock, and then after a second or two, unleashing a Tsunami onto the blazing van.

With the first whoosh the fire was out, but now George couldn't stop squirting, it went on for what seemed ages, and the girls had come back and got in the van by the time he had finished, I thought at one point, the fucking van was going to get washed away. Didn't really want one did he? I wouldn't like to be stood next him in the fucking bogs when he really did want one.

We all climbed back in to the van, which amazingly started first time, and continued on our journey to the gig, as I said before, these group vans knew their job and would usually get you to your destination, and although it sounds quite traumatic to have your vehicle on fire at the side of a busy road, there would never have been any thought about turning round and going back home, we just brush it to one side, and continued on to the club, 'the show must go on'.

We arrived at the venue, did our two spots uneventfully, then packed our gear away and set off for home. We'd just gone over the River Tyne, on the A1 when the van started playing up again, so it was decided that we would stop off at the Birtley service station, which was just past Gateshead, where the van finally gave up the ghost, and refused to budge any further. We all piled out of the van and into the service station restaurant, where we spent the full night waiting for assistance from one of our good friends back home on Teesside, who probably thought we were just a fucking bunch of pains in the arses. On the way back as we passed Sheraton Bank, at the point where George had swamped the road whilst extinguishing the van fire with his unstoppable deluge, the council had been out and put up some 'Danger Flood' signs; not really, I just made that bit up. We eventually got home at 7.30 in the morning, what a long night that was...phew!

18. The Standard

I n the early 70s, I was looking after a shop called Alleycats, where people would bring along things they had no use for any more, and we would buy them to sell on, hopefully making a bit of profit. We dealt with all kinds of things including antiques, but not what you would call real antiques, in fact I once bought a statue of the Venus de Milo before she lost her arms. Sometimes the shop was emptier than Joey Essex's head, but there was always the odd clever twat that would shout through the door when passing, 'what's new, fatty?' I've probably mentioned Alleycats before, and the fact that I lived above the shop, which was situated on West Dyke Road, Redcar, and directly opposite was The Royal Standard pub, known locally as The Standard. One night, around 1 am, I was woken up by loud voices arguing in the street outside, and as I looked out of the bedroom window, I could see a group of people on the other side of the road, in front of The Standard, engaged in a drunken brawl, a regular occurrence as it happened, and I was fucking sick of being constantly woken up in the middle of the night.

I went down stairs, and opened the front door to remonstrate with them but, after asking them to be quiet as it was one in the morning, all I got was, 'What's it got to do with you, fatty?' I thought, so much for Slimmer's World. 'Fuck off and mind your own business.' I didn't want to go over and join in the fisticuffs, after all we've all only got so much blood and I certainly had none to spare, on top of that I've never won any belts for boxing, and the only ones I've got now just to say keep my trousers up. No I only ever boxed once, that was in borstal and the guy hit me so hard I could faintly hear somebody counting to ten, then some sheep turned up and I fell back to sleep. Well, I'd had enough slaver from the fucking rabble across the road, so I picked up a milk bottle I'd put out to be collected in the morning, and flung it across the road towards them shouting, 'here's a bottle you won't like.' One of the voices shouted back, 'we'll get you three for that!' you three, he must have been pissed, I was on my own, apart from which he looked like he'd have to take his balls out to count to two, never mind fucking three.

Now I seemed to be getting nowhere with these arseholes, it was as if I was walking up a ship's gangplank with no ship at the end of it, so I lost it big time and picked up another milk bottle duly launching it in the direction of the mouthy twats on the other side of the road. Seeing what was coming their way, they all ducked, and the milk bottle flew straight through The Standard window, the part that said 'Royal'. The local police station was just around the corner, so it wasn't long before they showed up, and as I was already known to them, my protestations of innocence were to no avail, so I spent the rest of the night in a police cell.

It was noticeable that the pain of glass which bore the name 'Royal' was replaced with plain glass, so it now read only Standard. It was probably from that night on that it became known as The Standard and not The Royal Standard, who knows?

19. YER FUCKING JOKING AREN'T YER?

Some of the gags I got away with in the seventies
(By the seat of my pants)

I once worked with a bird impressionist, I said you're crap mate, so he flew off the handle.

I took a girl out to a Chinese restaurant; the waiter came over and asked for our order. She said, 'I'd like chicken and chips, please.' I said to the waiter, 'I'll have the same, how much is that?' He said, 'Twenty pounds.' I said, 'fucking hell, that's a lot for chicken and chips!' The Chinese waiter said, 'well, I chase after chicken, catch chicken, chop chicken's head off, pluck chicken, fry chicken, put chicken on plate, chips peas, ten pounds. Then I have to chase after another chicken, catch chicken, chop chicken's head off, pluck chicken, fry chicken, put chicken on plate, chips peas, another ten pounds; two chicken, twenty pounds.' I said, 'all right, chonk, whatever you say,' then turned to my date and said, 'what would you like to drink, pet?' She said, 'I'd like a cocktail, it's called a Horse's Neck.' I said, 'ok then, but I'll have its arse, I'm not paying for two fucking horses!'

I'm so unlucky, that I found a wage packet yesterday and, fuck me, the lazy bastard had only gone and had three days off.

There were two women talking over the garden fence. One said, 'do you know, I can never decide which part of the day is going to be best to hang my washing out to dry.' The other one said, 'why don't you do what I do; first thing on a morning, I pull the bed sheets back, and if my husbands willy is lying to the left, I hang my washing out in the morning, but if it's lying to the right, I hang it out in the afternoon.' The other woman said, 'what do you do if his willy's standing to attention pointing straight up towards the ceiling?' The reply was, 'nothing, who the fuck wants to wash on a day like that?'

I took a girl home the other night; after sex I said, 'in nine months time, you'll probably have a baby, you can call it Royston, if you like.' She replied with, 'well, in two weeks time you probably get a rash, you can call it measles if you like!'

I work harder than Esther Rantson's toothbrush.

The wife was on her death bed, she said, 'I have a confession to make, I've been unfaithful to you,' I said, 'I know, that's why I bastard poisoned you!'

I bought the wife a jaguar for Xmas, hope it rips her to fucking bits.

Girl said, 'guess how old I am, Roy, and you can fuck me,' I said, 'one hundred and six,' she said, 'near enough, go on then!'

The beer was so flat it was served in an envelope.

He might not have been a doctor, but you should see him operate.

The wife said, 'was I drunk last night,' I said, 'I know, I had to undress you,' she said, 'was I tight,' I said, 'well you were the first two times, pet.'

A funeral passed yesterday, she said, 'I wonder who's dead,' I said, 'I think it's the one in the box.'

'How did you get that hair style.' 'Try putting your finger in the light socket.'

I came home late and asked, 'is my dinner hot, pet?' she said, 'it will be if the bins on fire.'

'I met a girl while fishing.' 'Did you catch anything?' 'I'll know in a couple of days time.'

I've had this suit since it was a pair of gloves.

This is a hit song; when I sing it people hit me.

I'm not saying it was an old club, but the last comic was stoned to death.

20. NORth EaSt

Show-business is not all doom and gloom you know, you could say watching a stripper piss in the sink could be regarded as a bit of a bonus, in fact I said to one stripper, 'if I'd known you were going to do that, I'd have brought my washing with me.' It always brought a smile to my face when, as the stripper made her way to the front door, she would usually have to walk through the main concert room in among the lads who'd just watched her, as one in perfect harmony they would break into a rendering of 'we've seen your fanny, we've seen your fanny'; and they say culture is a thing of the past!

It was on a Sunday lunchtime that I was booked at Sunderland Boilermakers' Club with a couple of strippers, when a mass brawl broke out during my first spot which, in case you were wondering, had nothing to do with me on this occasion. But of course the headlines next day in *The Sunderland Echo* were, 'Geordie comic incites riot,' I'm not even a fucking Geordie. It took forty five minutes for the police to settle it down, while I had locked myself in the dressing room for safety, but this still didn't stop the fucking dozy concert chairman saying, 'Chubby, what about your second spot?' There's only so many ways you can say, 'go away you silly cunt,' but believe it or not, three months later there's a phone call asking me to go back to the same fucking club, I said, 'hang on a minute, I'm just looking for a cut-throat razor for my fucking wrists.'

Nineteen seventy to seventy one, I'm performing at the St. Peter's club at South Bank where, while I'm on stage doing my act, I see that my driver, Ronnie, is pointing to a girl. After coming off stage, he walked into the dressing room and couldn't wait to blurt out, 'phaaaw you lucky sod, there's a bird out there says she loves you Chubbs, and she's fucking gagging for it,' I said , 'bring her back here then, Ronnie.' Well, you wouldn't believe it, she was fucking frightening, she had a fringe with a bald patch, she was also as fat as fuck, and in fact she was the nearest living thing to Friar fucking Tuck that I'd ever seen. I said, 'Ronnie, I wouldn't fuck her with your cock,' then continued, 'look at her, she's mutton dressed as lamb, without the fucking mint sauce!' A half hour later, I was carrying my stuff down the fire escape at the back of the club, when I hear a noise, it's Ronnie, he's got his beer in one hand, with a ham sandwich in the other, and he's giving this fat lass a portion, and not of his ham sandwich either, because Ronnie was one of those lads who wouldn't part with fuck all. He shouts, 'Chubbs, do you want sloppy seconds?' I said, 'Ronnie she's a fucking pig, and anyway I'll get my own sandwich thank you, just get in the fucking van you dirty bastard!'

Newburn is a small settlement on the River Tyne, and the name of the pub escapes me at the moment, but I do remember that the place in question was heaving with drunks, there was even a fight going on in the car park as we arrived. The lad who'd organised this do, very kindly got me two beer crates to stand on in the corner, then Ronnie my driver, who was not the brightest spoon in the drawer, and had Van Gogh's ear, the missing one, for sussing a situation, started to set my gear up, which was two small Marshall speakers on stands.

I was escorted to a little room next to the bar, where, as I walked in, I heard someone sobbing, it was the stripper, she was well known on the circuit as 'Big Black Babs from Billingham', who hadn't inherited any beauty at all. 'What's wrong?' I asked, she said, 'I've done one dance, and as I bent over, the lads in the crowd were stubbing their fags out on my arse.' I wanted to say, 'is that because your minge is the same size as a fucking ash tray,' but there's a time and a place for comedy, and this wasn't one of them. I was beginning to think the time and the place for comedy wasn't out in the pub standing on two beer crates either, so I beckoned Ronnie over to the bar and said, 'take the speakers down, put them back in the car, because these people in here are fucking animals.'

Ronnie was a lovely lad, in fact he'd give you the shirt off his back, if it wasn't for all those spots, the spots on his back not his shirt, by the way. As he was taking the speakers down, the organiser asked him, 'what are you doing?' Ronnie quickly replied, 'Chubby said that these speakers aren't big enough, I have to put them back in the car and get the large ones out.' 'Oh, that's ok then, I'll give you a hand,' Ronnie said, 'no let me do it, because you're not insured, they are very expensive and if you drop one, we'll be in trouble.'

As I was stood in this small room, still trying to comfort 'Big Black Babs from Billingham', I heard a whistle and looked out of the window, it was Ronnie, he shouted up, 'the car's loaded, we're ready to go,' so instead of walking through this drunken haze of bastards, I climbed out of the window, jumped in the car and we fucked off as a quick as we could.

The next day I got a phone call from the organiser, he said, 'you crafty bastard, you fucked off sharpish, mind you, I have to admit you should have got a bravery award just for turning up in the first place. Poor Black Babs is still in that little dressing room now shaking and sobbing like fuck, I'm going to have to get a psychotherapist to talk her out of the fucking building!'

21. DOTS

Club acts, in the early days, had to rely on the accompaniment available at each venue where they were appearing, invariably each club would tell you they had the best organist and drummer in the area, 'oh, Fred and Vera, have been with us since the club opened, all the acts swear by them, swear at them more than fucking likely. Workingmen's Clubs would generally have had an upright piano which you could hardly hear over the rat-a-tat of the club drummer, who'd usually come straight to the club from his session with the boys' brigade.

Vera was a very good reader on the keyboards, in fact if a fly landed on her sheet of music she would play it as if it were a note, but the club had bought her a brand new organ with hundreds of knobs, the only thing it didn't do was make the tea, and the only knob she'd seen before was her old man's. I heard a committee man say to Vera, 'do us a favour, please stop sticking your music on our brand new organ with Blue Tac'. In those days I was performing my own songs like 'I'd use your shit for toothpaste', or the 'Cunt' song, and my favourite, 'My dog's got a bone and he's looking for a nice round arse'.

To give you some indication of what the drummer was like, he was wearing winkle picker shoes, and I'm more than certain that his previous job had been with Idi Amin's fucking firing squad. Anyway to start the nights entertainment Vera opened up with the tune '*Money can't buy me Love*' and the way she played it, it wouldn't have bought her a packet of fig fucking rolls, but never worry, it could be worse, because when I worked in Spain the backing was none existent, and in Switzerland, if you didn't yodel, you may as well just fuck off.

Although I played drums at the time, to begin with Allcock & Brown relied heavily on the club backing before we became a self-contained unit providing our own accompaniment. The club organist and drummer were more versed in providing the music for 50/50 dancing, waltzes, foxtrots (sounds uncomfortable), Eva three-step, etc., so on concert nights when they had to back the artistes, they were generally like a fish out of water. As far as the clubs were concerned, the main thing about their Fred and Vera was that they were cheap, but at some of the clubs in Scotland there'd be no organ at all, and some places just wouldn't fork out for a fucking organist anyway, we were regularly faced with being accompanied by someone playing the accordion, what a fucking nightmare!

It was not without its funny side though, I recall working at a club in Doncaster when, during our first act, I heard this peculiar sound coming from behind, and when I looked around, the drummer was actually playing a trumpet right in the middle of our show. I can't have been the first act to tell him that I was going to shove the trumpet so far up his arse, people would think he'd had his fucking lips enhanced, in fact if he'd gone any faster with his drumsticks, he would have started a fucking fire. I remember quite a bit back now, there wasn't much room on the stage to set all of our equipment up, and I was removing some items, when the club drummer said, 'you can't remove my kit,' I said, 'well, can you tell me where I'm going to set my drums up then?' He said, 'I'm telling you now mate, you are not removing my kit,' I said, 'well, you've got two choices pal, I either remove your kit, or your fucking teeth, it's up to you!' But it's unfair to say that club musicians were entirely of the same standard, some were even fucking worse, no truthfully, we did come across some very good musicians occasionally, few and far between as they were.

Now, because we wanted every chance available of getting decent backing for the act, we went to the expense of having our accompanying music written out professionally. We engaged the services of Mr Gordon Scurr, who was the M. D. (Musical Director) at one of our local night clubs, he was a brilliant musician, and was well known for producing first class 'dots', which was what musical manuscript, used in the workingmen's clubs, was affectionately known as by people in the business. You see to the uninitiated, the completed work just looked like a load of dots thrown randomly onto a sheet of paper, as if someone's fountain pen had been leaking. The work he did for us was excellent, and we thought that we should have no trouble now from anyone who could actually read them; what do you think?

We persevered with club backing, even though if we found a keyboard player who could actually read our beautifully written dots, then it was highly unlikely we would find a drummer who could, and with so many stops and starts in the act, it was vital we had a percussionist who could follow what we were doing. One night, we were on with a girl singer so we stood at the bar to watch her act, but the poor girl didn't stand a chance; the backing was atrocious, so bad I think the fucking organist had a pair of Siamese wrists that hadn't been separated at birth, and fuck me, the drummer sounded like my old grandad did when he was building his shed in the garden. We decided to take a chance and not use them at all that night; it was a turning point as we made a decision to become a fully self-contained unit from then on, so as not to have to rely on Fred and Vera ruining our act any more.

40 year old copy of Allcock & Brown dots found lurking in the loft

22. Wales

During my show-band days, we would regularly work the South Wales club circuit, touring for two or three weeks at a time, so it was vitally important that we had good digs to come back to each night after our shows. We'd set off in our little red post office van and, if you'd ever seen it, you must have thought we'd bought it off Dick Turpin at fucking gunpoint. There were rules and regulations regarding the van, farting was a definite no-no, our pet name for the van was the 'condom buggy' but so far it hadn't seen any action and was still a virgin. We hadn't realised Wales was so far away, so we ended up taking it in shifts to drive, but when we eventually got to Wales it seemed completely foreign to us, the villages were named by someone who should have been given the death penalty. We went through one village which was so unpronounceable, the guy who named it must have fell over carrying a box of fucking scrabble.

The arrangements for the digs were given to little Davy, one of the band members, and on arriving in Cardiff he realised he had left the details of the digs at home, so after he had plucked up the courage to tell us all what he'd done, we found ourselves high and dry, in what we thought was a foreign country, with nowhere to stay. Davy had a bright idea, he said, 'pull over at that telephone box,' at which point Davy told us that he remembered the woman's name was Mrs Jones. After going into the telephone box, which was obviously used as a night time toilet, I came out and said to him, 'just because you can do a hand stand in a fucking shoe box, Davy, doesn't mean you can also pull a random name out of a fucking telephone book,' then showed him the two phone books I'd brought out from the telephone box , one with everybody else's name in and the other one full of Joneses and I said, 'they must like sandwiches round here, they're all interbred.' Then after I'd smacked him over the head with the book full of Jones's we contacted the agent we were working for, who was able to put us in contact with the right Mrs Jones and enjoyed her wonderful hospitality for the duration of our stay.

The second time we went to Cardiff, we stayed in Cathedral Road, with an agent called Don Tyrer. What a character he was, he'd say, 'breakfast 8.30. don't be late,' so if you went down at twenty five past eight he'd say, 'too late, I've switched the pans off,' he was joking, of course. Don had collection of porno movies which would have got a vicar a hard on, and he had us in hysterics all the time. He once told us that he used to be a singer, I said, 'with that face, you should have become a fucking comic.'

George, Mick and I slept in one room, and when I woke up one morning Don was in bed next to me, completely starkers, he said, 'was that good for you, darling?' I leapt up, chased him along the landing, and wacked him with one of his own fucking flower vases shouting, 'you mucky cunt,' went back into our room where the lads were crying hysterically with laughter, then the next time I saw Don, I just said, 'I've had better!' Whilst there, we went for a look around the fabulous Cardiff Arms Park where I committed the ultimate sin by walking on to the grass. I must have only made one footprint on the hallowed turf when a very stern Welsh voice came over the tannoy, 'get off the grass, boyo,' well I shit myself, but apparently that's good for the grass anyway.

One of the clubs we would visit regularly was Tynewidd Labour Club, in Treherbert, set in the heads of the valleys. This club wasn't like just any old workingmen's club, and it was a gig that most acts looked forward to working. For starters it always had three acts on, so there was only ever one spot to do which for a workingmen's club was unique, these clubs usually wanted you to work your fucking balls off for as little money as they could get away with. It also had curtains on the stage that opened and closed, a novelty unheard of at most of the venues where we'd performed, but the main reason acts loved to go to this club was because of Emerice.

Emerice was the M.C. (Master of Ceremonies), we were used to being met by a committee man acting, begrudgingly, as Concert Chairman, not a real live compare like Emerice, he was quite different, as gay as they come he had obviously been in show-business for a number of years . I remember after setting up my drums, whilst sitting on my drum stool, he came and sat on my knee, I said, 'excuse me Emerice, I'm not the band's slut.' Tynewidd Labour Club was regarded so highly that the leek competition they had on during that day was able to attract the likes of Max Boyce to be one of the judges.

The introduction that Emerice would give you made you feel that you had already made the big time with all the superlatives he'd use to bring you on stage, in fact it made you wonder if he'd actually got the right fucking act. We looked out at the audience that night and I remember thinking, this must be where Hale and Pace got their idea from for The Management, because everybody was wearing a dickey-bow and a nice suit, I thought we must have been booked for some posh do. Anyway the first act did their spot, then it was time for the bingo, followed by a small period where people in the club were allowed time to recharge their drinks, after which Emerice came on to the stage and did his usual stylish chat, which was his way of settling the audience before the show started again, saying, 'we have a special treat for you tonight, it's been a long time since they have been to the club, I'd like you all to put your hands together and give real Tynewidd Labour club welcome to The Treorchy Male Voice Choir.' Then almost the whole fucking audience stood up and got on the stage, there was hardly anybody else left sitting down, all the suited gents sat in the audience were part of the Treorchy Male Voice Choir. After they had done their little stint they all left the club, so by the time we went on for our spot there was hardly anyone left in the club, the rest of the audience must have been family and friends of the choir, because they'd all fucked off home too.

Believe it or not, but it was a Welsh club which nearly stopped Allcock and Brown in its tracks before we got started. You see after deciding to form Allcock and Brown, it was thought that we would like to do our first gigs away from our native North East to see how it went, because we didn't want to die on our arse in our own backyard, little did we know that there'd be plenty of time for that later on. We contacted several agents and came up with a week doing the Workingmen's Clubs in South Wales, our first night being at Swansea Dockers' Club. We didn't know about the Dockers' Club reputation at that time, but anybody in the business reading this now will have just gone into a cold sweat at the mere mention of the name, especially if they are a comedy act.

We shared the bill with Johnny Goon Tweed, an impressionist who did all the voices from The Goon Shows, he was fantastic, but unfortunately got the usual Swansea Dockers' notorious reception, so you couldn't imagine our comedy going down, they might as well have held hands and had a séance to contact the living. We needed this gig like fucking Venice needed a road sweeper. Up the river without a paddle is probably the phrase I'm looking for, this was our very first booking with a new format and brand new untried material, it was like the lions verses the Christians at The Coliseum in Rome, very gladiatorial and there was only going to be one winner.

We were all for getting in the van and fucking off back home thinking we had made a big mistake, but decided to give it one more shot, so the next day we rehearsed in the digs to tighten the act up, taking out what we thought hadn't gone well at the Dockers' Club and moving a few things around. That night we were appearing at The Ringland's Social Club in Newport, and what a difference, we tore the roof in, had a great night and from then on in, we never looked back, unless of course someone was chasing us out of the club, which did still happen occasionally, call it an occupational hazard.

After that we flirted regularly with the Workingmen's Clubs and Night Clubs of South Wales acquiring a good reputation and following, but not everybody seemed to get what we were doing. We were asked to do a week for an agent called Peter Groves, and he booked us on, what turned out to be his own venue, The Candlelight Club in Llanelli. On the first night we put on our usual show which had been going down very well all over the region, but I have to tell you, our act at that time was a bit like Sticky Vicky's minge in Benidorm, a bit fishy and not for everybody.

It was early in the week, with not many people in the club, so the mild applause we got at the end of the show wasn't anything to write home about, and after we got off stage, changing back into our normal attire, the dressing room door opened and in walked Peter Groves the agent, and owner of the club. Not looking best pleased, he turned to me and said, in a rather effeminate voice 'you can't say shit on my club,' I said, 'I didn't say shit, I said shite.' Looking even more flustered by then, he said, 'you'll have to do something different, or you can't come back tomorrow night, can't you twizzle your drumsticks around your head or something?' looking directly at me again. Now Mick and George were looking extremely anxious in my direction, because it was becoming very apparent that, by now, there was only one place my drumsticks were going and that wasn't around my own fucking head.

We started going to Wales on a regular basis, and on one occasion, George took his brother along. We were staying at the Happy Valley Caravan Site in Porthcawl, when one night George's brother brought a girl back to the caravan, I have to say, you'd have needed chloroform to kiss her, he said, 'she's one in a million.' I said, 'a million, that's about the chance you've got of getting a fuck off her.' She mentioned that she had children, now I haven't a clue how many, but I can't count passed six, so I wouldn't really know. Then he announced he was going to marry her, I said, 'you've only known her a fucking hour.' We all said, 'come on, I mean we're not saying she would win a gurning competition.' Well, seeing as we were in the caravan, with the bunks very close together, there was only a curtain separating us, we never heard the word condom used, we never heard the word foreplay, but I'm sure I heard him say the word, 'oh yes, I've got a Porsche,' I didn't know Porsche made fucking bikes. I mean, we all like a fuck, but not in front of our mates, that caravan was going back and forth with such force, I was starting to feel sea sick and we were on dry land.

Yes those were the 'couldn't care less' days, when jokes were plentiful, but it was no good telling her that because she was a midget and they were going straight over her head. We could hear all the grunting and groaning. She said, 'you lot aren't laughing are you?' I said, 'no we're just trying to waft the flies away from your minge.' God, we had so much fun in Wales, I could actually move there, I've always thought that the Welsh think, 'well life's just something you have to put up with.'

Generally, our visits to South Wales were very well received, and we had some great times there, especially The Stoneleigh Club at Porthcawl, where we started the week as the supporting act and finished it Top of The Bill. Yes, South Wales was good for us, where else can you feel right at home sleeping in the back of a van, on top of a mountain surrounded by some rather good looking sheep?...Well, we had been away from home a long time!

23. The Sporty

After a gig, if we were working local, we'd often end up in The Sporting Club at South Bank, great place to wind down, and we got in for free because we were in the Musicians' Union, or at least the doormen thought we were. Got some great acts on there too, some of today's top entertainers first trod the boards at The Sporty, as we liked to call it. Being the only nightclub for miles, it attracted all sorts of different characters, even down to the lads on the door, but I still couldn't understand why all four bouncers were called killer. There was one, even in the middle of winter, who would stand there in just his vest, displaying a tattoo on his chest which said, 'who are you looking at, cunt face?', it should have carried on to say 'Welcome to the Sporty'.

I was standing at the bar the night Lonnie Donegan's bass player was arrested by the police, and taken away for none payment of maintenance; they could probably have arrested the rest of the blokes in there for exactly the same reason. As the police came in, you could see most of the lads scurrying around to hide in the first dark corner they could find. Yes, Crimewatch could have probably filmed their whole series here in one night. You really have to understand what this place was like; if they'd changed the name from Sporting Club to Zoo, it would still have been a great night out; they would have just been letting in a different type of animal.

Despite all of this there was a strict dress code, you had to wear a tie and your hair hadn't to be too long. The Sporty eventually burnt down, an arson attack allegedly, though it has been said that it wouldn't have done, only the doormen wouldn't let the firemen in without a tie on. Rosario's barber shop next door, used to stay open late in case anyone wanted a hair-cut, buy a tie, or maybe even something for the week-end, you see, at The Sporty, you were guaranteed a shag if you weren't too fussy.

I took a girl home, one night, from The Sporty and stopped opposite Lazenby village at a lay-by in a camper-van I'd borrowed from a mate. I kissed her, she said, 'what are you doing?' I said, 'I thought...' She said, 'oh! I'm not like that,' I asked, 'oh, right, have you never been with a man before?' She said, 'no, no, I haven't, no. 'You must be a virgin, then,' I said. 'What's one of them?' she asked. I explained to her what a virgin was, and her attitude suddenly changed. She said, 'you'll have to show me what to do, do you know where it goes?' I said, 'I think it's between your legs, pet' and then just got on with it, she was very keen and picked it up quite quickly, like an old pro.

Next night I'm stood at the bar in The Sporty when one of the lads asked, 'did you have a good night last night, Roy?' I said, 'yes, do you see that bird over there? She said she was a virgin until last night, in fact I even had to show her what to do.' The lads started crying with laughter, I said, 'what are you laughing at?' They said, 'we've all fucked her, she says the same thing to everyone!' Not long afterwards, one of the lads spotted the same bird in a girlie mag and brought it in, well there she was, legs at quarter to four with a gash like wizards sleeve. How the fuck did I let this slapper dupe me into believing she was a fucking virgin; I must say, it took a long time to live that one down.

They weren't all slags at the Sporty; I remember one classy bird saying to me, 'if you feed me, you can fuck me.' Now to be fair, at that time I wasn't one to give any of my food away for fuck all, so I took her home, made her a corn beef sandwich and shagged the arse off her. Afterwards I said to her, 'am I the first person you've slept with?' she said, 'you will be, if you go to sleep!' So I kicked her out; she wasn't getting fucking breakfast as well.

24. WACKY RACES

You really had to know my Uncle Arthur to understand why he'd asked for the song '*A pub with no Beer*' to be played at his funeral; if there had been a pub with no beer, it would have been because Uncle Arthur and my dad had supped it fucking dry. I'd asked George to come along for a bit of moral support, and on the day of his funeral we arrived at Eston cemetery before anyone else, half expecting the clouds to part with Uncle Arthurs distinctive voice bellowing out, 'you two are early aren't you?' but then we could have been on time and Uncle Arthur was actually late for his own fucking funeral. Being early gave us time to look at some of the gravestones. We didn't get out much, and as I've mentioned before we were in quite a rough area, so it was no surprise when I noticed one headstone had on it 'Goodbye you Old cunt' a sadly missed mother obviously. Then on another 'Dennis died suddenly eating pussy, choked on his wife's pubes', but I know what I'd like to see on my headstone, 'we've made a mistake, son, come back and consult your doctor.'

As we'd arrived at the cemetery in good time, we decided to park the van well out of the way, so as not to hinder the funeral procession after the service; at that time we were travelling to our gigs in the red post office van, a Morris 1000. The ceremony was to be held in a small chapel situated in the dead centre of the cemetery, dead centre, can't help it can I, then we had planned to sit at the back, leaving afterwards without attending the actual burial.

When we entered the Chapel, there was one young girl wearing a low cut top displaying a massive pair of bazookas, I did say to George, 'she probably thinks she has a divine right.' He said, 'her left isn't bad either.' I bumped into one of Uncle Arthur's old friends in the chapel, he said, 'hello Roy, haven't seen you for a while, where's your father?' I didn't say anything and just pointed upwards with my forefinger. 'Oh,' he said, 'I'm awful sorry to hear that, son, when did he die?' I said, 'he's not dead, he's up there pinching lead off the roof!' During the service the vicar spoke saying, 'Arthur was a good parishioner,' I thought, well this vicar can't be from around here then, because he obviously didn't know Uncle Arthur. Can't remember him ever setting foot in a church before, he wouldn't go anywhere he couldn't get a pint and a pickled egg.

It wasn't a classic service by any standards, but if God does exist I'm hoping that he has a good sense of humour, because I stole a Bible to take back to the van so I could use it to hold the passenger seat up and stop it from falling through the floor. I'd been chatting to one of Arthur's relatives in the chapel, he was wheezing so loud, I said, 'how old are you then?' he gasped, 'eighty nine,' I said, 'well it's a bit pointless you going home isn't it, mate? Just hang around here a bit longer and save yourself some fucking bus fare,'...Ah, ever the diplomat!

After the ceremony the funeral procession, led by the coffin, filed out of the chapel; being sat at the back we were the last out. We then made our way back to the van, which George was driving, and as we settled into our seats and turned on the engine, he looked in his rear view mirror and said 'I think we've got a problem here,' I said' 'why, what's up?' George said, 'the funeral processions right behind us,' I said, 'fuck me, let's just get going.' Now, don't forget we're in the middle of a cemetery, so getting our foot down was not a viable option, apart from the fact that getting our foot down in our van could cause it to go right through the fucking floor, but you tell me, what kind of cemetery has speed bumps, them hearses couldn't go any fucking slower if their breaks were locked on.

We moved off at a snail's pace, turning left at the first opportunity, but sure enough the hearse, which was now gaining on us, also turned left, we took a right, yes you've guessed, they did too. George said, 'don't worry Roy, there's a small roundabout coming up, I'll shake them off there.' Left we went, duly followed by the queue of cars, which now appeared as if they were looking for an opportunity to overtake. This was becoming quite farcical, and, even considering the sombre occasion, we just couldn't stop ourselves giggling like a couple of school kids, all it needed was some Benny Hill style music to finish it off.

Try as we might, the pursuing cortege was still following us, so much so, that eventually I turned towards George and said, 'they all must think we've got Uncle Arthur in the back of the fucking van.' Well that did it, there's the two of us driving ever so slowly around the maze which was Eston Cemetery, a string of cars copying our every move, with the thought that Uncle Arthur could be in the back of the van. We couldn't help ourselves bursting into hysterical laughter, and still do whenever the subject comes up; one thing's for certain though, I'm sure Uncle Arthur would have seen the funny side of it.

25. Fast Food

Travelling around as we did, often meant stopping off for a quick snack, and on one occasion we'd been on the road for quite a while, which meant the three of us, Mick, George, and me were starving hungry, so we decided to pull in to a service station. I always thought Mick and George had a built in dinner gong, and I've never seen two people eat so fast in all my life, whenever we sat down to eat anywhere, we'd have to ask for a bucket of cold water to be placed on the floor near the table, just so they could dip their knives and forks in to cool them down. I ordered three plates of egg and chips, plus bread and butter, and the fat bird at the till was so miserable, I'm sure that when they originally arrested the Yorkshire ripper, her name must have been written on a piece of paper in his pocket. She said, 'I'm sorry about the wait,' I misunderstood what she meant and said back, 'don't worry, pet, you can't help how heavy you are.'

As she put the meals down, George and Mick picked theirs up and went and found a table, I put the back of my hand on my egg, and said, 'can I ask you something, has the Pope given this egg the last rites?' The two lads were sat down by now tucking in so fast that they were probably warming their own food back up on the way to their greedy fucking traps , then they noticed I was still arguing at the till and both looked at each other as if to say, 'fucking hell, here we go again.' You see, Mick and George had seen all this before; if ever I wasn't happy with a meal, I would always complain quite vehemently, which usually ended with me being escorted off the premises under duress, they had left too many meals behind before and being as starving as they were, this wasn't going to be another one of those occasions if they could help it.

We'd already waited so fucking long for our meals that I thought we were going to have to leave a forwarding address, but we were so hungry, I was thinking now I know why Ozzy Osbourne bit the head off that fucking bat. I would never buy the lads baked beans because they were both big fans of Blazing Saddles and we had this agreement that there would be no farting in the van. The meal was a disgrace so I sent for the manager, when he came, he looked about six foot four with a nose like a blind cobbler's thumb, now I've learnt over the years to never pick a fight with someone who's so ugly that they've got fuck all to lose. I complained about the food, and then turned towards the lads to get their meals so I could give them back, but there was nothing left, they'd even eaten the fucking design off the plate. Both of them had been scoffing even faster than usual to make sure they'd finished their meals before the inevitable happened and I was asked to leave.

Anyway, after remonstrating even further, I was told that there was nothing wrong with their food and, if I didn't like it, to get out. So I shouted to the lads, come on we're getting out of this shithole, the foods crap and the robbing bastards won't even give me a fucking refund. Back in the van, both of them said quite tactlessly, 'by, I needed that, I was fucking starving,' knowing all the while that I'd had fuck all to eat. I was furious and said, 'I'm STILL fucking starving!' George said, 'don't worry, Roy, we'll soon be at the club, you can get yourself a packet of pork scratching there.' I said to Mick, 'for fucks sake, Mick, hold me back!'

We walked into a baker's shop in Rotherham one day, and I asked the girl behind the counter if she had a strawberry flange. Mick and George had already turned round and were walking towards the door even before the manageress had told me to get out of the shop or she'd call the police; no food again, then. I wouldn't care, if she'd showed me her strawberry flange, I'd have let her lick my cream horn.

Low Fell is an area of Gateshead, and when we worked the Tyneside area, we would often stop at the local Chinese Takeaway on the way home. The Chinese we always stopped at was called 'Low Fell Chinese Takeaway', and the very first time we went in, I asked the young Chinese lad behind the counter if Low was in; you see, being our first time in the area, I thought Low Fell was the name of the Chinese bloke who owned the place.

Mam as a young girl

Mam second from left with workmates

Mam, my sister Barbara and me

Family tea party

Where I lived as a kid

King Malcolm, Roy was on board for nine months

Drumming as a teenager

*Drawing talent
as a youngster*

Left: Early publicity photo

Below: Alcock and Brown

*New Faces
audition 1982*

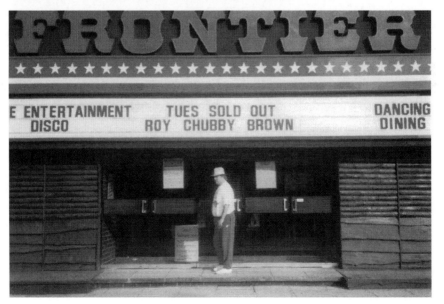

Batley Variety Club changes it's name to Frontier

With Billy Connelly

With Norman Wisdom

With Bernard Manning

Family photo

Not bad looking for sixty-five

Dancing with Jade Goody

26. Leicester

We were working the clubs in Leicester even before it became the capital of India, you see, in the 1950s when people weren't too bothered by immigration, Leicester seemed to be the place where all the Indians and Pakistanis went to live, in fact an Indian lady came over here, opened a sandwich shop and called it 'New Deli'. I was on stage one night, when I said to an Indian woman sitting near the front, 'have you ever been bed-ridden?' She said, 'yes, and on the back of a camel.'

We used to open our act with '*A boy named Sioux*', before we realised it was the wrong type of fucking Indian, but it was soon apparent that Indians like to enjoy a simple life, with their corner shop, a curry, and a Lamborghini or two. They don't spend money on essentials like we do, they just need a bit of fresh air, nor do they require home comforts, in fact some of them sleep on beds of nails, they are called fakirs, silly fakirs if you ask me.

We are talking about the days when nobody took offence or got upset about an off the cuff remark or a joke, so around this time I was able to talk about a Chinese man who'd had his head cut off, I'm not sure how it had happened, but I do remember being on stage and saying, 'I bet his mother's upset, she'd just bought him a new cap.' Yes those were the days when safe sex meant your girlfriends husband was on night shift.

We were working at a local club in Leicester when the dressing door suddenly opened and a guy stood in the doorway, 'who's giving comedy a bad name?' he asked, 'because that's my job,' it was Russ Abbot; Russ is a fantastic character actor and was a brilliant drummer too with his band The Black Abbots. They were appearing in Leicester at the same time as we were, and invited us to their show at The Bailey's Nightclub in the square. It was around the time that Brian Jones, guitarist with The Rolling Stones had died, and I said to Russ, 'I see Mick Jagger's lost a stone,' he looked at me and said, 'by you're fucking quick, aren't you?' I said, 'well I'm not the Big Issue seller Russ, he's outside.' We loved the Black Abbots' show, with Clive doing a rendition of '*Somewhere over the Rainbow*' which I still think is the best I've ever heard, and, of course, Russ was hilarious. After the show we got talking and, as they were staying nearby at The Holiday Inn, they asked us if we'd like to go back to the hotel for a nightcap, we had the basic prodigs to go back to, so we jumped at the chance.

Once in the hotel, we sat in the foyer drinking those small bottles of whisky and laughing and joking for what must have been hours. We could see it was getting light again outside, when one of the Black Abbots said, 'does anyone fancy a swim?' Well, by now, we were all blotto and in the mood to agree with anything, sounded like a great idea anyway, only thing was, because our prodigs didn't have a swimming pool, only a tin bath, none of us had brought any swimwear along, 'not a problem,' said one of the lads, 'we've got plenty.' So off we went to their rooms to get changed, I went to Russ's room; Russ didn't fancy a swim and was going straight to bed, so he lent me a very loud flowery pair of Bermuda shorts; I looked like an extra from the film *South Pacific*, without the fucking suntan. I folded my suit over one arm, carrying my glass of whisky, which I'd brought up from the bar, in the other hand, and then asked Russ how to get to the swimming pool where I was meeting the rest of the boys. He said, 'when you get in the lift press G that will take you to the pool.'

It was now around 6am, and you could physically feel the hotel waking up as I got in the lift, where after pressing G as instructed, it eventually stopped, and the doors opened, I then walked straight out...into the reception, which by now was milling with people, all of whom turned towards the lift to see me standing there, pissed off my face, wearing a pair of flowery Bermuda shorts, suit folded neatly over my left arm, carrying a glass of whisky in my other hand. I walked as best as I could straight to reception and asked, 'can you show me the way to the swimming pool, please?' The shocked receptionist simply said, 'it's downstairs in the basement,' now I'm still not sure if Russ knew exactly what he was doing, by directing me to the foyer looking like a prize prick.

Anyway once in the swimming pool, we had a great time with the rest of the Black Abbots. We had swimming races, where we would swim towards our drinks, balancing them precariously on the edge of the swimming pool, then becoming more boisterous, we started throwing the wrought iron pool-side furniture in and diving for it; health and safety would have had a field day, but they weren't there, so fuck 'em. We caught up with the lads a few times that week, and they came to watch our show one night, great lads they were.

Whilst in Leicester, we were working The Royal British Legion Club on a Sunday lunchtime, and some members of Show-addywaddy were in as the band originated from the area. We got talking, and as it was a Sunday afternoon in the early seventies, we were going to be at a loose end while waiting to go to our evening gig. One of the lads from the band gave us his front door key, told us to go and spend the afternoon at his gaff, and help ourselves to anything we wanted from the fridge. A real nice gesture, but if he's reading this now, after all these years it'll have finally dawned on him who broke into his house that long ago, and ate all his fucking food, I think we might owe him a bacon sandwich or two.

27. Rat-a-tat-tat

The band would stay overnight close to the venues we were working, often for a week or more, but the pro-digs that I remember most fondly were when we stayed at 1 Vasey street, Rotherham, memorable because that's my real name, Vasey, not Rotherham. The couple who ran the digs were called Alf and Mary, everybody who was anybody had stayed at these pro-digs, there were photos on the passage walls and in all the rooms of some of the acts who'd been, and there was a mina bird in the passageway, that made everyone laugh; sure he knew more swear words than I did. Mary had greeted us earlier by saying, we have six of you staying at the moment, so there'll have to be two sittings for breakfast, as we don't have enough cutlery, it keeps getting nicked.

Mary would leave sandwiches and a flask of coffee or tea for the acts when they returned back after doing their evening shows, apparently biscuits weren't allowed until your payment cheque had cleared at the bank. There was usually some cheap wine available, so cheap that when you took the cork out you could smell the Spanish grape-treader's feet, well that's who Alf used to blame. I'd always found in pro-digs that the toilet paper was usually rough, you might as well just use emery cloth on your arse, 'cos they'd already made emery cloths for dicks (Dick Emery) Bum-Bum. The first morning I foolishly said to Mary, 'I've been scratching all night, the bed must have fleas,' I was only joking, but left myself wide open, because without a seconds thought she came back with, 'maybe they're fans of yours, and you brought them with you.' No, I wouldn't say it was the cleanest of pro-digs we'd been to, in fact it hadn't gone unnoticed that there were mud-flaps on the fucking hoover.

The lads and I shared the flat in the attic right next to the water tank, so if anybody ran the water or the toilet, we would hear a loud flushing noise. Then on the second day, there was such a loud noise coming from downstairs...Bang, Bang, Bang, I embarrassingly said to Mary, 'is somebody building a shed below me?' she said, 'it's Mr Smith he has a wooden leg.

But this where my story really begins, because I got my own back, you see I'd bought myself a small electric piano with head phones, I think the first tune I ever learnt was *Stand up, Stand up for Jesus*', which now we've got Viagra, you don't need to sing any more, I would have taken violin lessons, but I wasn't sure which chin I should put it under. On this particular night, after we'd done our gig, I'd gone straight back to the digs on my own, Mick and George had stayed out and gone to a night club, nothing unusual there then. I suffer from insomnia occasionally, and this was one of those nights, so I sat up in bed playing my new keyboard with my headphones on, just tapping away quite merrily, now I must point out that I wasn't using a mallet, or playing '*Flight of the Bumble Bee*', the reason for mentioning that will become clearer later on.

When Mick and George returned to the digs in the early morning, clubs kicked out at 2 a.m. in those days, they unlocked the door and walked in, and as it was so early in the morning, they were being extra quiet, trying not to wake anybody up. They got inside and closed the door expecting it to be deathly silent, but instead they could hear a dull, rhythmical, rat-a-tap tapping noise resounding through the house, like a demented woodpecker on smack. They both stopped in their tracks and looked at each other, 'what the fucking hell's that?' said Mick, 'sounds like Long John Silver on a fucking pogo stick,' came the reply. As they started to climb the stairs, it was noticeable that the noise was getting louder; this was a three storey building, and we occupied the self-contained flat at the top. On the first landing, they were greeted by some very angry residents standing outside their bedroom doors, complaining like fuck because they were being kept awake. When they saw the lads, they had a right fucking go at them, because the sound seemed to be coming from upstairs, one said, 'have you got Pinocchio in your room having a wank? He sounds like he's going to set himself on fucking fire,'...everyone's a comedian.

The same thing happened on the second landing, with the tapping sound getting louder the higher they got, more bleary eyed guests were stood waiting to have a go at the lads, because by now it was pretty obvious where the noise was coming from. 'What the fuck's going on in your room?' asked one, 'fuck knows,' came the reply, 'we are as much in the dark as you,' the landing lights had been on a timer, and they'd just gone out.

So, Sir Edmund Hilary and Sherpa Tensing, or Laurel and Hardy, you decide, made the last push for the summit, which was our flat, still not knowing what the fuck the noise was. The flat door was opened very slowly, the living room was in darkness, but there was a bright light shining through from our communal bedroom. They tippy-toed in towards the bedroom, still the tapping continued, on reaching the bedroom, the door was ajar and the lads could see directly in. What they saw was a back view of me, sat up in bed wearing only my y-fronts and a pair of headphones, with my head swaying rhythmically from side to side. My head phones were plugged into my new electric keyboard, thinking no one else could hear me, but what I didn't know was that the constant thudding of my fingers on the keys were reverberating throughout the building.

They crept up behind me, stifling fits of the giggles, they were after all both pissed, and grabbed a headphone each. Well I nearly shit myself, 'What the fuck!' I said, not knowing who was behind me, 'you're keeping the whole fucking house awake,' said Mick, 'what do you mean?' I asked, 'everyone can hear you tapping out your tunes,' said George, 'they're all wide awake stood on the land-ing.' Of course, as I'd stopped playing, the tapping stopped, a loud cheer and applause came through the still open door, with a soli-tary voice shouting, 'thank fuck for that, we can all get some sleep, now!' The lads said, 'it's a bit late to be practicing, Roy, what tune are you learning?' I said, 'Silent fucking Night, what do you think?'

The next day was our last in Rotherham so, after breakfast, we started to collect our things to pack into our bags, with three young lads on the road there was stuff just laid about everywhere, we usually managed to find everything though. This morning was different, there was a pair of my socks missing, I'd looked every-where but to no avail, they would be easily spotted because they were bright yellow. Obviously the first thing I did was accuse one of the lads for nicking them, 'what the fuck would either of us want with a pair of your fucking smelly socks?' said one, he had a point, so I wrote them off as a lost item.

As we came down the stairs, Mary was waiting for us in the hallway to collect the remainder of our digs money; she always waited at the bottom of the stairs because too many of the fly-by-night acts had sneaked out without paying, giving her a fictitious forwarding address. As I was coughing up my hard earned lolly, I noticed something stood in the corner of the hallway near the front door, it was Alf's golf clubs, but what really drew my attention was the fact that all the irons did not have any covers on, but his two biggest woods had bright yellow covers. I got closer to them, and yes you've guessed, I realised the covers were my bright yellow socks, I thought what a cheeky, thieving cunt. There was nobody else in the hall now, so I took my socks off his clubs, bent his fucking 'mashie niblick' in half and disappeared through the front door, climbed in the van, and fucked off to our next town. I was fuming and couldn't stop going on about how this twat Alf must have come into our room, looking for something to cover his clubs with and noticed my socks on the floor, so he decided to nick them for his own good, one of the lads said, 'for fuck's sake, Roy, put a sock in it!.

28. That's Entertainment

Show-business people are very different from your average man in the street, and in the early seventies I'd meet up with other acts, after we'd finished our gigs, in The Contessa night club in Middlesbrough. It was small intimate club but it had a particular bar where we would congregate in order to discuss what had been happening to us all lately, drowning our sorrows from the night's events and talking about how many clubs we were taking to court to get our money...yeh...like we would!

There was a section in the car park outside, next to the disabled and the parent and child parks which was especially for emotionally disturbed comedians, and you certainly had to be there early to get a parking place, because it was full every night. These were the nights when you'd hear gems from comedians that would stay with you for a lifetime; I asked Pete Mitchell one night, 'where's the wife tonight, Pete?' he said, 'she'll be at home trying to defrost her fanny,' I said, 'Pete, your wife is a lovely girl, she wouldn't hurt a fly,' he said, 'that's right Chubbs, unless it was buzzing around her minge.' Now that's what you call lad's talk, but we had an understanding amongst ourselves of 'what was said in the Contessa, stayed in the Contessa,' sorry Pete!

You find in show-business when comedians work together, it's a bit like a gang bang, nobody wants to go first or last, but whether you're fiddling, fighting, or fucking, us comics all piss in the same pot. We will all, at some point, end up in Benidorm doing some seedy little bar, where you'd go on stage at twelve midnight, when the people in your audience would laugh if their arses were on fire. I know because I've done it, been there, worn the T-shirt and the fucking kiss me quick hat, though funnily enough I did enjoy it, that was mainly because it was full of English people who have great sense of humour. Where else in the world can you get a full English breakfast and burnt to death at the same time, all for three quid. I've been there a number of times now, yet I still can't work out how 'happy hour' in Benidorm lasts for at least half a day, must be something to do with the fucking clocks. Benidorm is probably the only place on the planet where you could witness whilst walking along the street, two big fat women looking at ladies underwear in a shop window, one saying to the other, 'Margaret, have you seen the price of that bra?' 'Seventy Euros, God, I'd let them swing first!'

29. YER FUCKING JOKING AREN'T YER?

Some of the gags I got away with in the Eighties
(By this time, who gave a shit)

Mrs Cannibal said to her husband, 'why don't you go out and get us something to eat,' they were watching people go past, when a beautiful girl with long blond hair, big tits and a nice plump arse walked round the corner. The son said, 'what about her, dad?' dad said, 'I have a better idea son, let's take her home and eat your mother.'

He wore a wig, but he kept it under his hat, and he believed in re-incarnation, for when he died he left everything to himself.

There's a mouse in the bread bin dear, she said, 'quick just shut it it'll starve to death.'

I used to work for the local doctor's surgery; I'd go round making people sick.

I loved her in her lemon dress, because it matched her teeth.

When I was at school, I was told that little girls were quiet as mice, sugar and spice and all things nice; that's bollocks, the truth is, they stink of piss, sagging arse and tits, and you're lucky if your dick fits.

I woke up in the hospital after an accident, copper said, 'did you give a lift home from the pub last night to a dark haired woman with blue eyes wearing a red dress?' He said, 'that woman was my wife, you must have been travelling fast, her thong was found in the glove compartment.'

Women say you will get good sex from a man if you give him a good meal, that's why I've been on minute rice this week.

Viagra stolen from chemist, police say suspect still at large, and probably getting larger by the minute.

The wife's so insensitive, she had me charged with rape because I didn't pull her nightie down when I had finished.

We are only together because of our star signs; I'm an Aquarian and she's an arsehole.

I first spotted her on television when Tarzan was giving her a banana.

Last night we had such a bad argument, that we both slept on the couch.

Unfortunately her double chin has a double chin.

She can't touch her toes because of her fat fucking belly.

She went horse riding and they had to put the horse down.

Her tampon's a King size mattress.

She said, 'how am I going to keep your beer cold,' I said, 'stand it next to your heart.'

Wise man says, 'never play leap frog with a puff.'

Pussy? I couldn't get a fuck off a baboon carrying a lorry load of bananas.

I'm so unattractive, that whilst in the church choir, the priest never looked at me once.

She was that sex mad, she had love bites on her piles.

30. Stampie's

When I first went solo, if there was a gig I didn't fancy, I'd suddenly get a really bad sore throat and ring my agent to tell him I was too ill to work, and one such occasion was a Friday afternoon booking at a local club called Stamps. I'd worked on the club before, it was always a tough gig and didn't pay very much, so I phoned my agent to tell him I was ever so croaky, and gave a performance over the phone that must have been worthy of an Oscar. I'm sure he knew what was going on, but accepted the fact that I wasn't going to do the booking.

It was the agent's task to phone Stamps Club and inform the owner of the situation. Now the club was named after the owner, Stuart Stamp, and although he was a mate, he was also someone you wouldn't want to get on the wrong side of, so after being told that I would not be coming, and not being one to mince his words, he went fucking ape-shit. He said, 'I've got a room full of suits, who've booked the club for a works function, especially to see Roy 'Chubby' Brown, and I have to tell them he isn't coming, they'll fucking lynch me.'

In an attempt to calm Mr Stamp down, the agent, in a trembling voice, told him he would ring around and try to find him a suitable replacement. A number of contacts were rung without any success; you see, either the comics available had worked the venue before and had a similar response, or they were reluctant to be my stand in.

It was starting to get desperate, then with the agent running out of possibilities, a young up and coming comedy act called Brodie Fry agreed to cover the gig. Brodie did a mixture of comedy and magic, but lived in Peterlee, so it would take him about thirty to forty minutes to get to the club.

The agent rang Stuart to give him the good news. 'Fucking good news?' said Stu, not having calmed down yet from receiving the previous bad news, 'I'll give you fucking good news. My suited audience is starting to get very restless, so this Brodie fucking Fry of yours had better be fucking good. 'I'm sure you won't be disappointed,' came the rather high pitched reply from the agent.

Job done, thinks agent, and breathes a sigh of relief to get Mr Stamp off the phone, lies back in his chair with his feet on the table, feeling quite smug having solved a tricky situation.

About one and a half hours later, the telephone rang, which it consistently does in an agents' office, but this time on the other end of the line was a very loud Stuart Stamp. Before anything else could be said, Stuart blasted down the phone, 'where the fuck did you dig this useless twat up?'

'What do you mean Stu, he's a good act,' whimpered the agent, 'a fucking good act? I don't think you'd know a fucking good act if one bit you on the fucking arse,' bellowed Stu, the phone almost melting in the agent's hand.

The agent then plucked up the courage to say, 'it happens with all comedians, usually they do a great show, but sometimes an audience doesn't take to him at all.' 'That's not what I'm bothered about,' said Stu, his voice becoming more agitated with every additional word, 'what I am bothered about is that he's just got the company's Managing Director on stage and cut his fucking tie in half. I've dragged him off stage and now I'm left with a hostile audience and a Managing Director with a two piece fucking tie, what's more they are all demanding their fucking money back.'

Agent says, 'I've seen the tie trick before, and the tie usually ends up back in one piece.' 'Well not this fucking time it didn't, he's fucked off now, but if I'd caught him, I'd have shoved these two pieces of tie right up his fucking arse. Tell him he's getting no fucking money, because I have to buy a new silk tie for a very angry Managing Director,' then with one last roar of disapproval, slammed the phone down.

Anyway, the agent phoned me up to tell me what had happened. When I picked up the phone, I didn't know who was ringing me, so I forgot to put on my croaky voice. The agent said, 'by your voice has had a miraculous recovery, Roy, have you been gargling?' I said, 'yes T.C.P., fucking good stuff, isn't it?'

31. Concert Chairmen

It's strange how, over the years, concert secretaries and chairmen brag about who's been on their club, the times I've heard, 'See that toilet?...Tom Jones had a shite in there,' or 'see that sink?... Shirley Bassey pissed in there, in fact Shirley stopped back for a drink with us, right up until 2 a.m.' I remember saying to him, 'was she a big spender?' he went, 'no, we got the round in,' obviously the joke went right over his fucking head.

Being the Concert Chairman in charge of the entertainment for a social or workingmen's club could be a thankless job, because if the acts were not up to standard or just not going down well, which was not always the acts fault, the chairman would usually get it in the neck from the club members sitting in the audience. Occasionally, because of this, the job often fell to someone who wasn't the sharpest tool in the box, if you get my drift.

One night I was on with a ventriloquist and we'd both done a spot each before the bingo. During the break, after announcing that the next night's entertainment was 'Norfolk and Good', the Concert Chairman came into the dressing room and said to the ventriloquist, 'can you hold your dummy a bit closer to the micro-phone please, because everyone's saying they can't quite hear him?' Well, we both creased up laughing, and the look on the dummy's face was picture. Then the chairman went on to tell us that the following week he had booked an act called Vince Eager and the

Clockwork Toys, a very popular attraction, but he was worried that the people at the back wouldn't be able to see the clockwork toys; what he hadn't worked out was that The Clockwork Toys was the name of Vince Eager's backing band. After the chairman left the dressing room, the ventriloquist's dummy turned his head to us both and said, 'daft cunt.' (Well he would have, if he could have!)

32. You can't please all of the people all of the time

'm not easily shocked, but when I found out Little Richard was gay, I thought, 'oh' that's probably what he meant by Tootie-Frootie, the title of one of his biggest hits, and I'm not so quick on the uptake either, because I had to think really hard when someone said to me as we arrived in Australia that it was tomorrow already.

Can I ask you, if you have ever wanted to punch a wall, because I often read things about me that I'm supposed to have said or done, written by newspaper reporters, and they're just ridiculous? It's pretty obvious that you can't do my job without being occasionally controversial, and I'm not afraid to share my opinions or to be interviewed. Though what I really like to concentrate on the most, is sticking to my own act, but being in the spotlight means you're an easy target for anything that could make a headline, truthful or not. I read somewhere not long ago, 'well, he's no Bobby Thompson,' Bobby was a top Geordie comic, sadly no longer with us, and I agree that I'm no Bobby Thompson because I've never tried to be like him. Bobby was a national treasure, and I've only got a sunken chest, well it tapers away from my belly, and he was acceptable with people and places where my material would have been totally out of place, but times change and by the seventies you would hear concert chairmen saying things like, 'why don't you book Chubby

Brown he fills the club and you can get him for the price of a good meal in Bangladesh.'

So now, the same reporters that were intent on misquoting me in their papers were coming to see me in these clubs, asking, 'what are you doing to fill these clubs? Can we take a photo of you?' I'd say, 'why do you want my photo, is it for your fucking dartboard?' The bottom line is you need broad shoulders in this business, people are rarely totally satisfied, I heard someone say Norman Wisdom laughs at his own jokes, so I said, 'mate, Norman Wisdom was the greatest clown that ever lived, that was all part of his act, and he would underline that fact by always finishing with his trade-mark song, 'Don't laugh at me because I'm a fool', are you thick or just plain fucking stupid?' No, there have been bigger stars than me who have had go through their careers with the understanding that 'you can't please all the people all the time!'

A comedian in 1935 called George Broby said, 'boys and girls, this is harmless vulgarity, friendly smut, and if you don't like it, you know where the door is.' You just can't analyse humour, there are so many different types of jokes that come to you on a daily basis, in fact everybody seems to make a contribution, whether they realise it or not, I think I must get away with it because I've got a fat face, and fat arse. I read only recently that, as you get older, you have to decide which of those two features you want to preserve, your face or your arse, you can't have both; well having embraced that report to preserve my good looks, I've a also been able to keep my trade mark fat arse, so up yours!

I was watching a programme taking an in-depth look at comedy history on channel four, and they were saying that they'd found what must have been the first ever joke book written way back in the twelfth century, I thought, 'you're having a laugh aren't you?' It was written by Monks but apparently, they didn't make a habit of it; the archives show that all the jokes were filthy and blue, so now you know where I get mine, from in fact it made me think that I should hire a Monk or two as script writers, because if it was good enough for Friar Tuck then it has to be good enough for me.

Have you ever wondered why one comedian can tell a story without getting a laugh, then another comedian tells the same story and people will fall off their chair in hysterics? It's simply because of the way it is told, so I decided to not only create an act but also an image to go with it, then after years of tweaking and experimenting I found that it worked. The only thing you have to live with is that some people think that the image you portray on stage is the real you, but I promise you it isn't; we do look a bit like each other though, but I'm working on that.

33. Knicker dropper glory

One Boxing Day night, I got a local gig at Old Thornaby Social Club, I always tried to get local jobs at Christmas time, and when I got there, I was pleased to see I was on with Gladys Ford. Now Gladys was a proper old school variety entertainer, with her act consisting of standard songs from over the years, a few comedy routines, together with a certain amount of audience participation, and she always got a warm reception whenever she appeared in any of the North Eastern clubs. Part of her act, during one of her songs, was to remove her knickers, always a big drawer, but don't get too excited lads, Gladys would wear about fifty pairs (exadge), and her husband was always with her to keep count as they came off, to make sure she didn't flash her bare arse to the audience. As she sang she'd remove a pair, then another pair and so on, and to add a bit extra spice to this episode, Gladys would ask a male member of the audience to come on stage and help her perform her knicker removing routine.

On this occasion Gladys asked an elderly chap who was sat near the front with his wife, to help her; it was quite obvious he was only too eager to be of assistance, belying his age by leaping from his seat, and bounding onto the stage like a gazelle. Now, before the spectacle of removing the knickers, Gladys would produce a plastic tube about a yard long in a 'u' shape, then from behind she would push it between the gent's legs, pointing it upwards, saying, 'Saturday night,' then pointing it downwards she would say, 'Sunday morning,' always got a laugh. This time when she pointed it downwards and said, 'Sunday morning,' a rather loud raucous voice came from the audience; it was the old man's wife, 'oh,' she said, 'he likes Sunday mornings.' 'Why does he like Sunday mornings?' inquired Gladys, 'because he gets his hole!' shouted his wife, so everyone in the club could hear. There was a moment where the room went deathly quiet, then as one, the whole audience cheered and laughed uncontrollably. Like the trooper she was, Gladys carried on with the rest of her show, but honestly, how do you follow that?

34. Stand up and be counted

Britain's Got Talent is one way of becoming famous, but serving you're time is another, then finding your van on bricks when you come outside of the club because you've said the wrong thing; it's called 'Treading the Boards'. This industry is full of young people who travel around with their mothers and fathers. But as soon as they're old enough to go out on their own, and have to face that enormous world of show-business, that's when the tears start, because it takes years and years of hard work to become an 'overnight success'.

You can bump into some pretty unpleasant characters at times, I've seen me holding concert chairmen up by the throat, just to get my twenty quid, but as they say, two days are never the same. I went to a Birmingham club for to do a charity event; I do charity gigs because it makes you feel good about yourself, but also helps good causes. The club was called 'The Flamingo' and I decided to go to the Albany Hotel which was just across the road, where I find myself still in the bar at one o'clock, talking to a very interesting gent. You know when you've seen someone before, but you can't quite remember their name, this person turned out to be Ludovic Kennedy, the famous broadcaster, who was there to prove that the Birmingham bombers were innocent, and the outcome was that they were innocent, and he proved it. Yes that hour I sat with him was the most interesting conversation I've ever had in my life, because, over the years, I've learnt to accept other peoples' points of view, but what I liked most about this fellow was that he was asking about me too. 'Oh,' I said, 'I'm at that stage of my career where I'm reaching the dizzy heights of show-business, with suggestive material.' I said, 'it's not stardom, but that's not what I'm looking for, I just like to work hard,' he then asked, 'did you take after your father?' I said, 'oh no, dad was a drinker, he liked a few pints.'

After years of working hard on the art of telling jokes, improving my timing and writing material, you know you're getting a little bit better when your money goes up a fiver, and doesn't that feel like sweet revenge? All those clubs that had paid me off in the seventies were asking for me to go back now, I was no longer just the filthy comic, in fact I was Roy Chubby Brown who could demand...yes, wait for it £200.00 per show. No more having to look around to find that every time you close your wallet you trap some concert chairman's fucking fingers in it, but of course there were still times when everything went wrong, like the time I got a rash off my inflatable doll, just another daft joke, no wonder my dog packed his bags and threatened to fuck off!

I have to say, that one of the nicest compliments I have ever had, was when I went to Norman Collier's funeral where we were all meeting up in a pub before going to the church. I was standing at one end of the bar, while most of the other celebrities were at the other end when suddenly a voice said to me, 'hi Chubbs', it was Bobby Knutt, comedian from Sheffield, 'why aren't you stood with the rest of them?' 'Bobby,' I said, 'in all honesty, you've got at least twenty T.V. shows over there amongst themselves, they all work for I.T.V. or B.B.C. and know each other very well.' He looked at me and said, 'you know, Chubby, they'd all love to be like you because if any one of them had the balls to say that word 'fuck', then their careers would be history. In this business you have to start off how you mean to go on, and be true to yourself, that's exactly what you've done,' I thought what a nice fellow, and what a lovely compliment. Anyway we both decided to get pissed, but the trouble was, on discovering the price of the drinks we both said, 'ah, think we'll leave it for another night.' I remember thinking at the time, I'd just been given a compliment for using the same word that got me a smack round the head off my dad...fuck!

I was asked to appear on the comedy quiz show 'They think it's all over', and I agreed to go on, but a month went by and I asked my manager why I hadn't heard anything yet, 'Oh,' he said, 'I received a letter from the producer, apparently you're not every-one's cup of tea and Jonathan Ross won't work with you.' I'm not sure whether that's true or not, but if it is it's funny how someone else can put the fucking spoke in for you, isn't it?

Later I was offered a part in a new drama series, and I remember going for the audition, where the producer said, 'can you remove your hat, because we'd like to see your face?' Fat lot of good that did because the programme didn't even make the T. V., but I'd always worn a hat, even at school where I wore my dad's hat, which was so big you could never see my face, and I couldn't see where I was going. That was a big turning point in my career, from that day on the hat stays; book Roy Chubby Brown, and you're also booking the hat, might be a different hat from time to time, but a hats a hat, and that's that!

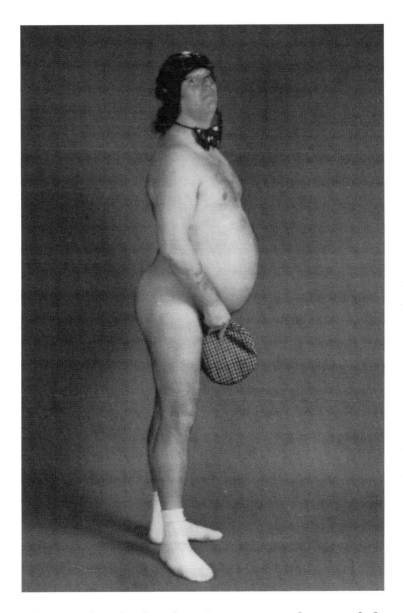

I removed my hat but the series was never shown...why?

35. XMAS DAY WITH FLOPPY the Rabbit

I had a cousin, Joyce, who was in a wheelchair and lived in a disabled centre called Blenheim House, in Thornaby. The lady, who ran the centre, asked me if I would do twenty minutes for the residents sometime over the Christmas period, and of course I said that I would. On the day of the show I arrived, but walking through the front door something smacked me straight in the face, the strongest smell of human shit you would ever encounter, and the temperature was in the eighties, as were the women who lived there, so the shit smell seemed even worse. There was a big fuss going on over a ninety-nine-year old woman in a wheelchair, who'd apparently got lock-jaw eating an ice cream, how the fuck do you do that? Believe it or not, it was a fucking ninety-nine, same as her age, wonder if she had any thousands and one sprinkled on, or does she have to wait a few more years for that?

Thirty children had been invited to this Christmas do, I heard somebody shout,' Thomas has swallowed a crayon,' and I said, 'I thought he looked a funny colour,' not a fucking titter, I thought this is going to be tough. Because of the kids, they had invited another act to appear, it was Harold from Hartlepool, with Fluffy the Rabbit. The guy with the rabbit started his act, but at least ten of these kids must have seen him before, because every time he did a routine, they were shouting out the punch lines, and finishing it off, I felt really sorry for him because he was being barracked by eight, ten and twelve year olds, it was so funny to watch though, and he didn't do very long. Just before he finished he said, 'ladies and gentlemen, boys and girls, I'd just like to wish you a very merry Christmas, and I hope Santa Claus poisons most of these little bastards,' then before the audience had time to realise what he'd just said, he continued, 'I've been Harold, this has been Fluffy the Rabbit, and that lad there in the red top has been a cunt, I wish you all goodbye,' then just turned and walked off, well I'm telling you I couldn't get my fucking breath for laughing, if I hadn't seen it with my own eyes, I would never have believed it!

36. NORth Of the BORdeR

've had to deal with some right dip-shits in the past, like when I first went to Scotland and they hated me. I'd be getting booed in the car park whilst getting my gear out of the car, while in one particular club which will remain nameless, Cowdenbeath Workingmen's Club, I walked through the door to see that the lady accordionist not only had a five o'clock shadow, but her face looked like a smacked yard of tripe, and she played the accordion so badly that the mice under the stage were wearing fucking earplugs. It was a Sunday dinnertime and most of the members were given a whisky and water as they walked through the door, and when I looked at the audience, believe me, they made those fellows in Braveheart look like fucking cissies. In a broad Scottish accent the accordionist said, 'have yea nay got nay dots?' I thought she said spots, so I pulled my shirt up and said, 'nay, not one'.

Eventually I was 'paid off', when we say 'paid off' in our business, we don't mean you get any money, like fuck, you're lucky to get away with just a good hiding. I, sheepishly, made my way to the next club, which was at Shotts, in Lanarkshire, where I was greeted with, 'are you an English cunt?' I of course replied, 'no, Pakistani. Silly fucking porridge-sucking, cable-tossing, bastard, I then said, 'did they make the movie "Chain Saw, fucking massacre here?"' He looked at me and went, 'no, I think that was in Texas', sometimes I wonder whether I should fucking bother. There was a big sign in the dressing room saying, 'you walk off at your own risk.' I was thinking my meagre fee might have to been used to pay for the pane of glass I'd have to break to get out of the fucking window. I did 45 minutes, and it was so quiet I could hear the hairs on the back of my neck growing, then afterwards, while I was having a pint at the bar, the chairman came over and said, 'would you go on and do your next 45?' I looked at him and said, 'are you related to two short fucking planks?' God, I thought Swansea Dockers' Club was hard, with its hairy arsed stevedores, because when I was there they were chanting in unison, 'kill, kill, kill'. Good singers, the Welsh.

37. YER FUCKING JOKING AREN'T YER?

Some of the gags I got away with in the Nineties
(By this time, I could say what I fucking liked)

The wife said after we'd finished our meal in a restaurant, 'shall we go dutch,' I said, 'fuck off, you've eaten more than me.'

Vaginas can't be that attractive, as soon as my bell-end saw one, it backed into it's tube.

Just come out of hospital, because neighbour's wife was sewing a button on the fly of my trousers, as she bent down to bite the cotton off, her husband walked in.

I'm as sick as a puff getting lock jaw on Valentine's Day.

Kids are like farts, you can stand your own but nobody elses.

The wife left me leaving a little note, saying, 'I love anal,' the dyslexic cunt meant I love Alan.

I'm only alive today, because my best friend's wife found those lumps in my testicles.

I've learnt a lot from women, that if you don't want a fuck, and she wants a fuck, you'd better fuck her, or you won't be fucking for a long time.

I never close my eyes during love making, because I did it once, and when I opened them again, she'd been gone half an hour.

I'm a domestic husband, I know how to turn on a dish washer, a hoover, and a washer at the same time, you just have to lick her clit.

Police were at the door this morning, the neighbour's reported that your wife screamed, 'she does officer during sex, especially when I walk in on her.

I must have the laziest wife in the world, even this morning I had to shout downstairs, 'this arse won't wipe itself.'

Suspicious, I accidentally knocked her handbag over, and birth pills fell out. I had a vasectomy last year, hope she has her next period in a shark tank.

She's had more hands up her dress than Miss Piggy.

I call her Tesco legs, open twenty-four hours.

I normally couldn't get a fuck off Anne Franks two minutes after she left the attic.

Took one girl home, had to have her brother with her, fucking conjoined twins.

Used to get stacks of pussy, when I had a tazer gun, not so much these day as rape whistles have got louder.

Girl said, 'I don't give a blow job, until I've known a boy six months,' I said, 'ok, I'll ring you nearer the time.'

The girl was covered in bruises from where the lads had been touching her with a twelve foot barge pole.

We called her easy jet, because she went all the way for nine quid.

Never lie to a woman, I never thought in my wildest dreams she'd want to see my Bat Cave.

You know your marriage is finished, when she tapes over your wedding video.

We now have separate beds, mines in Newcastle and hers is in Glasgow.

38. Club Fiesta

We do end up in some predicaments, I was standing at the bar in The Club Fiesta, Stockton-on-Tees, with a pint, and a brandy and coke, The Club Fiesta was a cabaret venue where all the biggest names of the time would appear, Tommy Cooper, Bob Monkhouse etc. There was a big titted barmaid giving me the eye, and I didn't have a partner or a girlfriend then. In fact I was going out with my wrist at the time, but even that turned out to be a right tosser. She said, 'would you like to come back to mine for a drink?' Bearing in mind it's now two o'clock in the morning. I'm not usually very observant, but even I could see she was gagging for it because she was rubbing herself like a dog with fleas, and it seemed she wasn't too bothered who she got gagged off with, I must have just turned up at the right time. Off we went, and within minutes of entering her flat, yet another word I like to use for fanny, I said, 'why don't you move your arse up and down?' She said, 'you know, all the lads say that,' at which point I quickly sobered up and said, 'must dash, darling, I've left a pan on the stove,' Then I slipped out of her flat through the back door, which was wide open, before I caught anything I might regret, I hadn't even got a stove, or a pan, phew!

39. BLACKPOOL

I've been working in Blackpool since 1985, so I'm known in some circles as Mr Blackpool, but I'd already done some part-time seasonal work there when I was only fifteen, working at the Fun House. I used to hand little mats out to the youngsters as they went down the slide, but I got caught charging them a tanner, two and a half pence to you, which put me on a bit of a slippery slope. I did all sorts of things back then, I sold deck chairs at one stage which is not good business in the winter, or even in some of the shit summers we had at that time either. It's hard to believe that, after all this time, my poster's are on billboards and buses all over Blackpool, only this time they weren't put up by the police.

By the way, Blackpool now has it's own fashion police, and I'm sure I don't have to explain to you how all the young ones walk around there these days, in fact if a girl faints, the paramedic wouldn't need to loosen her clothing, because she was probably wearing next to fuck all anyway. Someone was telling me that a copper had said to this particular woman, 'you're indecently dressed and I'm arresting you,' only for the 'woman' to say back, 'you'd better fuck off mate, I'm not a woman under these clothes, I'm a St Helen's prop forward, and this is my weekend clobber,' so the outcome was on that night, it was the copper that needed a fucking paramedic.

In the early days I used to meet up with other acts in a cafe on Station Road, where egg and chips was 1s 6d, showing my age now, mind you I think she charged two bob for the knife, fork and plate. You had to eat in because she'd keep the door locked until you paid her, then search you on the way out to see if you were nicking the salt and pepper pots. I think the little fat waitress, who was built like a fortress, must have fancied me because she would always say, 'will there be anything else, sir?' I always used to think, 'I'm sure there could be, darling,' I'd fuck anything in those days.

I got fixed up once, with a holidaymaker, now I wouldn't say she was easy, but instead of her hat saying 'Kiss me Quick', it said 'Fuck me slowly'. I took her back to my hotel thinking we'll make Blackpool rock tonight pet, then I asked her, 'what do you like the most about Blackpool,' she said, 'I like all the rides, but I've never had the Big One.' I thought, you're going to be unlucky tonight as well, darling! It was also in Blackpool where I met a tramp and gave her a fiver, then we bumped into each other again and I forked out a ten spot, in the end I married her, it was fucking cheaper. I hadn't been working Blackpool that long, so the venues I worked tended to put me on at twelve o'clock midnight, just to help clear the room.

On my second season I decided to rent a flat up near the Pleasure Beach, and on a morning, because I thought I was George Best, I'd run along the beach with a plastic ball. One particular day, I was running past a parked ice-cream van, when I spotted this fellow getting a cornet and I looked straight at him, I thought I know that face even though he had disguised himself by not wearing his wig. It was Paul Daniels, he looked at me and I looked at him, I knew him because one of my friends lived in Pym Street at South Bank, Middlesbrough, just three doors from his house. Of course I knew his accent straight away because we come from the same area, and there was no mistake, though he didn't know me from Adam, but I don't even know Adam either, so we had something in common. I watched closely to see if he pulled a rabbit out of his cornet or cut it in half and put back together again, but I must admit, after a few licks it did disappear...that's magic!

I'd been to see his show a few years earlier on the North Pier, I remember on the night, it was blowing a gale and pouring with rain and, when I got into the theatre, to say the audience was sparse would have been an understate-ment. The manager said, 'hi, Chubby, do you know Paul?' I said I've met him once, but that was a long time ago,' then as I looked around the room, I said, 'I hope he can pull a fucking audience out of a hat,' he pissed himself.

40. Sheree

I was standing at the bar of the Viking in Blackpool, one night, when a fellow comedian friend of mine walked in with a girl, he said, 'this is Sheree.' She was quite attractive, but a bit on the plump side, and I remember thinking, 'God, if you'd been a turkey, you could have fed a family of twelve,' but hey, I need talk. I asked, 'would you two like a drink?' he said, 'she can't, she's just come out of re-hab,' I said, 'oh, drank too much has she?' he said, 'no, it's drugs, Chubbs,' I thought, it obviously wasn't fucking slimming pills.

Then, out of the blue, he said, 'can I borrow your car tomorrow, Sheree hasn't seen her mother for six years, and I'd like to take her around?' I'm thinking, where's around, could be as far as Manchester, that's a hundred mile round trip? So I said, 'listen, you're not insured to drive my car, why don't I drop you off?' he said, 'that would be great, thanks.' Cutting a long story short, which isn't the best way of filling a book I know, but the next morning I picked them up at a boarding house. 'Right, Sheree, where does your mam live?' said I, 'Fleetwood,' was the reply. Fleetwood's only three miles away, I remember thinking, couldn't you get the fucking bus, you lazy cunt. If you've ever been to Fleetwood, it's quaint in some ways, with hundreds of rows of terraced houses painted different colours. We pulled up outside a yellow door, now you wouldn't give two pounds for the whole house, never mind the fucking door. I said, 'do you want me to wait for you?' my pal said, 'would you, Chubbs? Thanks mate,' I said, 'I'll go for a cup of tea somewhere, and come back when you're ready to go.'

This is where my pal takes up the story: - She popped her head round the door, 'yoo-hoo!' said Sheree, expecting the whole family to jump up in excited derision, her mother said, 'who is it?' she gave out another tuneful, 'Sheree.' 'What do you want?' enquired mother, 'I haven't seen you for about six years,' the tone not being what Sheree had hoped for. 'Well, I know that.' Sheree said, 'I've got a boyfriend, now, and his mate has a car, so we thought we'd come round and see you all.' Mother said, rather sarcastically, 'well, I suppose you'd better put the kettle on, if you can remember where it is.' Now, I'm not sure what kind of a welcome Sheree was expecting, but this certainly was not a *'Surprise, Surprise'* moment, our Cilla was definitely not going to spring out from behind the settee in this house.

Just then, a big fellow walked downstairs, apparently he was Sheree's brother, he plonked himself right next to me on the settee, and asked, 'who are you?' I said, 'I'm a friend of Sheree's,' 'What the fuck have you brought her here for, she's now't but a fuck-ing nuisance,' quizzed the brother, in an aggressive manner. Then, without any warning, while Sheree's filling the kettle, her mother shouts, nonchalantly 'by the way, your dad's dead.' Sheree said, 'eh?' 'Your dad's dead!' Sheree said, 'how was he?' The mother stormed back, 'never you mind, it's none of your business, got fuck all to do with you, you were nowhere to be seen!'...♫Surprise, surprise, the unexpected hits you between the eyes♫...probably be another six years before Sheree plans her next visit. When he told me the story, I just cried laughing.

41. Les

I t was noticable that most of the comedy stars from the sixties and seventies, had a couple of Rolls Royces, a Jaguar or a Mercedes. That was never my style, and it was never Les Dawson's style either, you see Les was one of the nicest people I ever met in show business, with no sign of bigheadedness, a complete professional. He never blew a line and never failed to deliver a joke to perfection, and I was lucky enough to have him as a friend. While standing at the bar one night, he told me how his piano routine came about, he accidentally played out of tune because he'd had a drink, and the people laughed so much that he built on it and a comedy legend was born. Les gave me a great review, he told everybody, 'this guy's comic timing is impeccable, if he could only just stop fucking effing and jeffing. Les told me he liked Ken Goodwin, I said, 'isn't he the one who laughs at his own jokes?' Les said, 'well, somebody has to.'

LES DAWSON

42. PUt DOWNS

Part of a comedian's learning code is 'To die gracefully' on stage, and in some cases comedy talent goes right out of the window, what you need then is bottle and backbone, the old Dunkirk spirit and some nifty footwork to get out of the road of any flying objects; the comedian has his own ammunition though, these missiles are what we laughingly call 'Put Downs', and they can penetrate the thickest skin or head.

So here's an example of just some of the Put Downs I've used over the years:-

1. When you got that face, did you get a receipt, so you can get your fucking money back?
2. Hope you bought two seats, you fat fucker!
3. Now, try saying that with your fucking mouth!
4. Put your head against that wall, 'cos that's fucking plastered too!
5. Go take your face for a shit!
6. When you were born did your brains stick to your mother's piss flaps?

To have a rapport with somebody in the audience can be hilarious, but then again it can be life threatening, I was recently confronted by a massive woman at the front of the audience shouting fat bastard, so I said to her, 'God, you need fucking talk, you must think "fat bastard" every morning when you look in the fucking mirror. Why don't you go home, take the needle out of your arm, and shave your tits? You'd need to have a fucking bag over your head just to get back scuttled, and by the way that's a lovely dress you're wearing, get a bargain from Oxfam did we?' The audience were crying with laughter, and that's always what a comic sets out to do; if these people decide to take on someone like myself, then they have to be able to take the consequences. But It was bad news for the fucking hippopotamus in the front row because she was now looking for a hole to crawl in, it would have had to have been a fucking big hole might I add. Most of these hecklers usually think they're more important than you, but the smaller the heck-ler, the bigger their egos tend to be, then there's usually only one result; total fucking verbal annihilation...serves themselves right for trying to spoil the night for everyone else!

43. Pete 'Chubby' Richardson

Peter who used to drive for me is a funny man, and on one Saturday in Blackpool it was raining, now that is a surprise, raining in Blackpool, that's why the traffic wardens have fucking webbed feet. I remember being dead chuffed because my name was on the side of all of the trams going up and down the prom advertising my show. In Blackpool, at this particular time, there was a variety of working class people on their annual holidays, we used to call it factory fortnight. There'd be pigeons flying overhead looking for their owners, probably going to drop a present from above for leaving them at home alone; that must be why they all wear flat caps!

Because it was raining, Pete was in the amusement arcade on a slot machine, which was paying out four pence for every two you put in. Now, Pete's well known for 'ow't for now't, give us a shout', so we stood there for two hours just to make six fucking quid. Pete had been shopping and had bought some gloves and a daft hat, but when we went back to Bisham, which was where we were staying, they both got left on the tram. Pete said, 'I'll go and see if I can find them,' I said 'Pete, it's only a hat and gloves, where are you going to look?' Pete said, 'the tram that we were on had your name on the side,' as did just about every other fucking tram in Blackpool! I just said, 'well fucking good luck then!'

We were driving back to Teesside that night, minus the hat and fucking gloves by the way, and on the way home we stopped at a curry house in Kirby Stephen. While we were eating our curry some kids came over on bikes, 'hey mister, are you Chubby Brown?' I was sat in the passenger seat next to Pete, so I said, 'yes he is, lads,' 'Can we have your autograph?' asked one of them, 'course you can,' said I, 'Chubby, give all those kids your autograph.' So there's Pete signing autographs because I wanted to finish my curry while it was still hot, cold curry for Pete; well if you see the photograph, he does look a bit like me.

One particular day we arrived at a hotel and the two girls at the reception desk said, 'hello, Mr Brown,' Pete said, 'hello,' I began to giggle. Pete played along with this, then turned to me and said, 'hey, Roy, get the bags,' which I duly did, placing the bags on a trolley and then standing to watch Pete imitating me. The girl asked him to fill out a form, but the form required information only known to me, so Pete turns to me and says, 'blooming hell, my minds gone blank, what's your registration and home number again?' which I gave him, then he said, 'oh, I need your gold card and number now,' to which I replied, 'hey, and I think you can fuck right off now!'

44. ROOT OF ALL EVIL

The only time I thought about money was when my ex-wife turned up at court for a divorce looking dead sexy, but to me she would have looked better if she'd had a Doberman Pincher clinging to her back. For legal reasons we'll just refer to her as 'S' from now on, and no that's not 'S' for sexy! When a woman accuses you of something you have to prove that you didn't do it. You have to prove it never happened, and I've learnt that lawyers make a deal amongst themselves without considering how the fuck it affects you. I did have a nice sticker in the back of my car saying 'Honk if you've fucked Chubby's Wife'; some people inherit money, some people earn money, and others are just solicitors.

All I ever wanted was a round of applause after giving her a decent fuck, but she couldn't even bring herself to do that. Anyway I said I'll divorce you with pleasure, she said, 'I'm afraid, pleasure will cost you extra.' I wouldn't care, I obeyed all the rules, I was only allowed to answer her back from Spain or anywhere a reasonable distance away. Fancy me marrying a woman who couldn't take a joke, one day she said, 'are you a man or a mouse?' I was tucking into a big block of cheese at the time and I said, 'I'm not sure but there's been a cat following me about all day, with its mouth watering'. Do you know she accused me of being an idiot? she said, 'you should see a psychiatrist, do you hear voices in your head?' I said, 'Yes, but only when I'm on the phone.' I knew she

didn't like me because the first time I asked for her name she said, 'it's in the phone book, find it yourself.'

    'S' differed an awful lot to me, she wanted a church wedding and I just wanted to call it off altogether, but we can all make a mistake, that's why they put rubbers on the ends of pencils. Do you know, there was nothing I wouldn't do for her, and there was nothing she wouldn't do for me; yes, we went through our entire marriage doing fuck all for each other. People took an instant dislike to her, mainly because it saved time, she once said to me, 'everybody hates me, don't they?' I said, 'don't be silly, everybody hasn't fucking met you yet!' She said, 'sometimes I just wish I could put my finger on it why everybody just walks away from me,' I said, 'maybe it's because you're fucking breathing!'

I once left her at Tenerife airport, after something she said about my family, and she could be so in your face, in fact she wouldn't be frightened to tell Roy Keane to fuck off. There were times when I'd pick up stuff while we were shopping in the super-market, she'd say to me, 'put that back, we don't need it,' just like you would to a naughty child, try as I might I could never get away with sneaking rat poison into the shopping trolley. She was so different from the lovely wife I have now, nineteen years, and we haven't had an argument, she gives me a mucky look now and then when I haven't done the house work right, or I've burnt her toast, but she's so kind, considerate and passionate, and has the patience of a saint with our kids, but she's blond, so it'll be no surprise when I tell you that she asks me questions like, 'you know these battery hens, Roy, how long do the batteries last?'

I'm sure if the Gestapo had still been around today, 'S' would have been a Commander in Chief, a fucking frightening one at that. She once fell off a ladder, I thought, I know what's going to happen here, the police will come round and say that I pushed her, so I quickly ran downstairs and shoved a shammy leather in her hand, to make it look like she'd been cleaning the windows. On our wedding day, her mother took me into the back kitchen and said, 'you do know what you're doing?' I said, 'I think so.' 'This is our 'S' we're talking about,' she continued. So I said, 'well, every-body deserves a chance.' Her mother said, 'she's a handful.' I said, 'well that's unlucky for me because I don't have very big hands.' If somebody had told me in those days, your wife's just told the Pope to fuck off, I wouldn't have been surprised. Anyway I managed to get away from her, when I told her my real name was Peter Sutcliffe, she said, 'I though you must have been a serial killer, when you said you could murder a bowl of cornflakes,' always had to have the last fucking word.

45. WOY

remember going to a club where the guy in charge kept calling me Woy, because he had a short tongue, 'lithen Woy, we thtart at eight o'clock, you do an hour, then we have bingo, followed by the waffle, then the girl thinger.' He thounded just like Elmer Fudd, who was an American cartoon character in the *Bugs Bunny* movies. I can't remember his real name so I'll call him Elmer from now, he told me my last spot was at ten o'clock so I said, 'hey I'm a comedian, not a fucking night watchman.' Elmer told me the girl's last number was going to be '*I will Survive*,' well, I took one look round the room and thought, 'not in this fucking shithouse, you won't.' You wouldn't have needed any laxatives after performing in front of this crowd, I was shitting myself at the way the audience looked, with their broken noses and tattoos, and that was just the fucking girls. A bravery award should be presented to anybody with the balls to get up on this stage even just to sweep it never mind perform, you see the Blood-tub had a bit, sorry I'll correct myself there, it had a lot of a reputation.

After first letting the audience know that sausage wolls and wissoles are sold behind the bar, Elmer finally announced me, 'the moment you've all been waiting for Woy Chubby Bwown, fwom Wedcar.' Well I'd been on stage about five minutes, almost a record for this club, and as usual nobody's watching me, this time they were looking out of the windows, because 600 yards away there was a house on fire, and you could see the glow a mile off. The audience were all just stood with their pints in their hands as if it was an everyday occurrence, so over the microphone I said, 'oh, this is fine, isn't it? I'm cracking jokes, and you lot are watching some fucker burn to death,' I said, 'Arthur Brown must be on over, road singing his bit hit 'Fire, I want you to Burn' is he?' I'm sure you've gathered that nobody laughed, in fact nobody laughed at the rest of my act either, but once I was in the safe haven of the dressing room, chairman short-tongue himself, Elmer came out with 'fucking marvellous, fucking marvellous, did well Woy.' I said, 'ahem, how do you know that?' he said, 'because nobody threw any dwinks at you,' thank fuck they were too busy watching the fire.

As you can see these clubs I performed in certainly weren't all wine and roses, in fact I worked one at Saltburn, with a bloke sat at the front shouting, 'your mother's a cunt fatty, your mother's a cunt fatty.' After about ten minutes of this I was fucking raging so said, 'would you like the microphone, sir?' He said, 'no thanks.' So I told him, 'well, you're fucking getting it, mate,' and smacked him right over the head with it; I was left standing next to him with just the wires in my hand, the microphone had disintegrated on impact. No messing, two bouncers came across, lifted him out of his seat and threw him out of the door. I shouted to them, 'you were a bit late, lads, weren't you?' I went to see about my money and the owner said, 'well listen, Chubbs, your fee was twenty-five quid, and the mike was twenty-five quid, so let's call it quits.'

When I came out of the club, the guy that I hit is sat propped up against a tree still unconscious, I said to one of the bouncers 'what's he doing there?' The bouncer replied, 'he's the fucker that couldn't take your joke.' I said, 'I know that but don't you think you should get him an ambulance?' It had been raining, and the blood had washed off his head and onto his suit, you'd think he'd been hit by a fucking J.C.B. not a microphone. Anyway I drove along the road, stopped at a phone box and rang the emergency services saying, 'can I have an ambulance please, I'm here at Saltburn walking my dog, and I've just come across a young man sat beside a tree, looks like he's been hurt.' The lady on the other end asked, 'can I have your name, please?' 'Yes," I told her, ' it's James Posthlewaite.' And your address, sir?' '3, Milbank Terrace, South Bank,' knowing fine well that a month earlier Milbank Terrace had been pulled down by the council for renovation.

It was Christmas Eve, and I was booked on Guisborough Quiot club, I was on with an act that was so bad that, while he was getting his gear in, people were already kicking him in the emergency doors. You see he'd been on the club before, and the club members had remembered him. Poor lad was waste high in bruises, where the fucking audience had been trying to trip him up, I'm sure this must have been the night he started drinking heavily. I was talking to the chairman and said, 'has he been here before?' 'Yes son, and he's crap.' 'So why did you book him again?' I asked. 'I couldn't get anybody else at this late stage.' Well after he had performed two numbers, with his guitar embarrassingly of tune, and his voice even worse, the crowd, not showing any Christmas spirit started booing, and the chairman closed the curtains on him, a pretty obvious sign in some clubs that you are paid off.

When we were all in the dressing room, the chairman came in 'sorry mate, you haven't improved one ha'peth, I'm paying you off.' I said, 'hang on a minute, it's Christmas Eve, he's probably got a wife and kids waiting for him at home, can't you give him

a chance? If you pay him off, I'm walking out of the club too.'
Chairman said, 'oh, if you are so fucking flush, why don't you pay
him?' putting me right on the spot. I didn't want to back down, so
I said rather relutantly, 'well yes, that's alright I will,' then took a
hundred pounds out of my pocket and gave it to this cunt. Calling
him such because he went and got straight into his car and fucked
off, and all the time I was thinking that once the chairman had
gone out of the room, he'd give me the money back. You know I
never saw that act ever again, so instead of being on a hundred and
fifty pounds that night, I was now on fifty. Six months later and
I'm on the same club with two strippers, the chairman said, 'by the
way, the strippers are crap.' I said, 'don't start that fucking game
again, I'm not going to be caught out this time, you can pay for
the fucking strippers yourself, good, bad or in fucking indifferent!'

An agent once booked me at an old folks' home, where I
didn't raise a fucking titter, so I rang the agent and said, 'I've just
been talking to the matron, at the old folks' home you sent me to,
she's the lady who took the booking, and said she had told you
that most of the residents are deaf and dumb.' The agent said, 'yes,
I know that, I thought it would be good for your act.' I wouldn't
care but the only sign language I know is the one I used to use to
say goodnight to the foreman when I had a proper job all those
years ago.

I could easily have become disillusioned whilst doing stand
up in the early part of my career, because my comedy spot would
always be after the raffle, the bingo, and then the monthly draw,
and if that didn't tell you where the club's priorities were, then
nothing would. Being told, 'now, hinny, you go on after the bingo
and the meat draw, but most of them will have fucked off home

by then, anyway,' was often the catalyst for a heated disagreement with the concert chairman about the running order. As I've said before, I would have so many arguments with these people, one even grabbed me by the throat, so I pushed him down the stairs where he landed on the bingo machine and squashed his balls. But he was lucky enough to break his fall when he landed on his bulging wallet, which was as fat as fuck from all the back-handers he'd been pilfering, the only thing that was really hurt was his pride. After an incident like that it would have been easier to knit tar or find Lord Lucan's ashes than get paid, not because I'd assaulted the concert chairman, but because I'd broken the fucking bingo machine.

Yes, I've had more slanging matches with committee men than you could shake a drumstick at, there were chairmen in charge of looking after the acts who didn't have any respect, noticeably for girl singers especially. On arriving at a club, they'd often say, 'now then mate, I'm going to put you on after the tart singer, or the fat bird chanter,' or I've even heard said, 'you're on after the floozy with the big tits.' Now if half of these girls had heard those conversations, I'm sure they'd just get straight back in the car and fuck right off, especially the floozy with the big tits!'

46. Chubby by Name (Chubby by Nature)

’ve been reading recently, that five pieces of fruit a day, plus exercise, gives you a longer, healthier life; ah well, that's me fucked. Anyway I've rung the fish and chip shop and asked them to bar me out, and I'm also going to give up pork pies, I thought if the wife can give up smoking, then I can give up pork pies, so I'm going to do exactly what she did when she reduced her smoking; I'm just going to have one pork pie after each meal. I think that giving up all the things you enjoy, like your favourite food, and torturing yourself with extra physical exertion doesn't actually extend your life, it just makes it seem fucking longer. The one thing about being overweight is that you know that everybody else who's overweight is as unhappy about it as you are, so I thought I'd better do something about it, and I recently went for a check up at the well man clinic. The doctor told me that my cholesterol level was higher than Blackpool Tower, which was upsetting on two levels; one is my high blood pressure, and the other one is I haven't got a head for heights, I said to the doctor, 'I was once told I had the blood pressure of a 29-year-old.' 'Oh,' he said, 'when was that?' I said, 'when I was six.'

I don't know if you've ever eaten in America, but the amount of food they serve up on your plate is quite unbelievable. When Helen and I arrived in Vegas we were so hungry that we went straight to a restaurant, you see there's an eight hour time difference, and we thought we should to catch up on some shut eye, as they say over there, but needed a light meal before we went to beds, so we ordered burger, chips and a salad for each of us. When they brought the salad in a tureen we thought it must be between us, but then they brought another one together with a large bucket of French Fries. Fuck me, all I can say is, if I'd eaten that lot and gone to the bog, I'd have definitely splashed the back of my fucking neck, and by the time we had finished our meal we could hardly walk. Just a warning though: they say you can always tell a bad cafe because they'll own a fat dog, the waitress will have spots, and the bill will be under a quid, with a free sick bag on the way out. I began to eat well when I started making a couple of bob, but that doesn't mean I don't have salt, pepper and vinegar on my fish and chips, with an extra portion of mushy peas, you've still got to continue enjoying life's luxuries. I've come to the conclusion that the only way I'll lose weight is by having a leg off, or both, so I can't get to the fucking fridge, but that probably won't work either, because I'll just fall over and rock myself to sleep. I don't ask for much in life really, in fact I'd be chuffed to bits if I could just find a belt and tie that fits, because whenever I buy them I always have to return them to the shop because they're too tight. I've tried the aerobics classes, and found it difficult to concentrate with all those young birds bending over in front of you, in fact when I went to a class to try it out, I told one young girl, 'look, if you keep doing that right in front of me, pet, you'll be getting a taste of my celery stick a lot fucking quicker than the one you brought to eat.'

As Confucius would say: it's not much fun if you can't put your socks on because your belly gets in the way, but it's ok if you can't put your socks on because your bell-end gets in the way.

47. YER FUCKING JOKING AREN'T YER?

Some of the gags I got away with in the Noughties
(By Now, I gave my audience what they came to expect)

Wife said, 'my head's all over the place,' I said, 'it was pointless buying that guillotine then.'

Spent ten minutes with Jordan, yesterday, I realised two things, firstly her tits aren't as big as you think they are, and secondly the staff at Madam Tussaud's haven't got a sense of humour.

Went to the doctor's with what I thought was ring worm on my stomach, the doctor said, 'you're fine, Mr Brown, but the next time you back-scuttle your wife, tell her to give her arse a wash first.'

Bloke went into the library and asked if they had any books on suicide, the librarian said, 'we did but they never get brought back.'

Girl said to me, 'would you like a blow job, Chubbs?' I said, 'yes please, as long as it doesn't affect my invalidity allowance.'

Wife said, 'before I met you, my stars said that I would meet somebody tall, dark and handsome; they got your fucking weight wrong as well.'

I thought I'd get a fiver tattooed on my bell-end, just to see how quickly I can blow my money.

You know you've been together too long when your wife gets a beer belly and you still find her attractive.

They say, never go to bed on an argument; we haven't slept for two years.

My ex-wife was so fat on our wedding day that the photograph fell off the wall.

I said to this girl, 'where have you been all my life?' She replied well, for most of it, I was teething.'

She's had three husbands, but only two of them were her own.

My first wife was a nurse in the X-ray department, but she soon saw through me.

A chap said to me, 'are these all your kids or is it a school picnic?' I said, 'no, they are all my kids, and believe me, it's no picnic.'

I went to see a private doctor, he said, 'I'll examine you for £200,' I said, 'that's good, if you find it we'll have £100 each.

We went to a nudist camp, she said, 'is that Dick Brown over there?' I said, 'yes, we've had a lovely summer.'

Prostitute went to the doctor's, he said, 'you're very ill, don't go to bed for a few days.'

Dad was a shift worker, if you mentioned work, he'd shift.

Life is like pubic hair on a toilet seat, sooner or later you'll get pissed off.

He's so unlucky, that when he went on a smash and grab raid, he got caught pinching the brick.

She was a very good swimmer; she'd have to be, because she was a call girl in Venice.

A friend said, 'can I tap you for a tenner?' I said, 'for a tenner you could hit me with a fucking brick.'

I said to a lady with three sets of twins, 'do you always have twins?' she said, 'oh no, sometimes we have sex and nothing happens at all.'

48. The Big 'O'

As I say on stage boys and girls, I never trusted girls, especially the ones that picked you out of a police line-up, and as young lad I could swear the Pope must have been getting more fucks than I was. I found girls very strange creatures, but there was one girl in Blackpool who said, 'if you get my name tattooed on your body, I'll get your name tattooed on my body. After about ten pints of beer, I thought that sounds like a good idea so I said, 'ok then, what's your name?' she said, 'Elizabeth, Susan, Anne,' I said, 'hang on a minute, sounds like I'm getting the raw end of the deal here because my names Roy, and if you have it tattooed across your fanny, you'll save money on the 'O'.'

GIRL WITH THE TATTOO.

49. The POOL

We arrived at the back of a club in Liverpool, to be greeted by a small group of young lads who started to mill around the van while we were taking the gear out and carrying it into the club. After we'd emptied the van, locked the doors, and started to walk towards the club, one of the lads approached us and said, in his broad scouse accent, 'if you give us 50p, we'll look after your van, mister.' What he really meant was, if you don't give us 50p, we'll slash all your tyres and put your fucking windows through as well, so we gave them 50p for their endeavour, and to make sure our van stayed in one piece while we were in the club.

The first time I did Beeches Club, at Aintree Racecourse, the owner of the club, John, was a wonderful fellow. I remember arriving at the club, and the cloakroom girl smiling at me, I said, 'hello, I'm Chubby Brown.' She said, 'Oh...ahem... I'll get John for you.' I exchanged pleasantries with her, and then at the end of the night, she said, 'are you doing two nights?' I said, 'yes, I am,' she said 'would you like to go for a bite to eat, to a Chinese?' I said, 'yes, that would be lovely.' John said to me, 'be careful, Chubbs,' I said, 'what do you mean?' he repeated himself, 'just be careful,' sounded to me like this man obviously knew something I didn't, but I took her to the Chinese all the same. She had some fucking appetite, ordering just about everything off the menu, I'm thinking there goes my first nights fee, this had better be worth it.

The next night, I arrived at the club, where John takes me into his office and says, 'how did you get on, last night?' I said, 'oh, it was alright, you know,' 'Well listen, I like you Chubbs,' said John, 'so I think I should show you something,' and he pulled out some photographs...well, there's my cloakroom attendant, face twisted in an evil position, sucking what I can only describe as a fucking barge pole.

Yes, there was my lovely, with such a large cock in her mouth that even I was getting a semi on, but fucking hell there was more, the next photograph, showed her bent over a desk, in my favourite position but with someone else stood behind her, yes I knew it wasn't me straight away, because you can't even rent those cocks out. I said to John, 'she's not the shy type then, is she?' The photographs were so clear I could see her dry skin and spotty arse, together with the semen stains around her fanny. I don't know what I'd said the night before but, after the show, she was waiting at the door for me with her coat on, so I went out the back door, jumped in my car with my suitcase and fucked off driving like mad, thinking about what a lucky escape I'd just had. I'd left her a message with a barman saying, 'please tell the girl I had crabs, and I didn't want to give them to her,' then walked out sideways via the back entrance.

50. A TRIP to Malta

When we went to Malta and arriving in August of that year, we endured a white knuckle taxi ride from the airport. The driver was flying down these badly maintained roads, doing what seemed to be twice the speed limit, when we could see we were approaching a roundabout; incidentally in Malta, they drive on the same side of the road as we do. Fuck me, there was no question of him slowing down, in fact I think he went faster the nearer we got to the roundabout, then as we approached the roundabout he didn't look right or anywhere, he just shot straight out into the traffic, we were shitting ourselves, but what we didn't know was that in Malta the traffic which is already on the roundabout stops to give way to any car that wants to join the flow of traffic, our hearts were beating ten to the fucking dozen, and we'd only just arrived.

It was 114 degrees in the shade, but as my mother used to say, 'well keep out of the shade then,' it was that hot we were choking on the dust, and I could feel my contact lenses melting, in my eye sockets. I was newly married, but by now my wife and I weren't even on farting terms; anyway we jumped on a single decked green bus going into Valletta, and went to the square. Arriving in Valletta, we sat outside at a table belonging to a very old cafeteria, in fact if you looked down from the table, you could tell how old it was because it must have been in the same position for such a long time that there was ivy growing up the legs. When we ordered two coffees, the waiter was delighted to tell us that the Pope had just been to Malta, I said, 'he must be promoting a new album, is he?' But after making a remark like that, it wouldn't have surprised me if he had spit in my coffee, the Maltese take their religion very seriously indeed.

I asked the couple on the next table, 'where's the best place for us to visit?' and this typical Englishman replied, 'go to the Blue Lagoon, there's a fantastic chip van that pulls up there.' Hundreds of birds, including seagulls and pigeons, were flying overhead shitting on anybody that passed, then flying at the table and pinching the sugar, while we were cleaning their shit off our shirts. A young lad, I would guess to be about ten years old, stopped on his bike, pretended to walk past the cafe but simply grabbed a pigeon and necked it, quickly putting it in a carrier bag, then jumping back on his bike and peddling off, as if it were an everyday occurrence. It was witnessed with quite a bit of shock by everyone sat in the courtyard, in fact my wife said, 'you know what's caused that, all the violence on television.' I said, 'darling, there's violence everywhere, the Nazi's didn't have fucking television,' and they say wives keep you young at heart, if that's the case, then I think I should still be at fucking school.

Well, you wouldn't believe in a million years what happened next, a refuse disposal lorry stopped on the other side of the square, and this guy looked over at me and shouted out in broken English, 'Chubby, Chubby Brown', and within seconds there were fifty pairs of eyes staring straight at me, and no I hadn't just taken the lid off a can of sardines. I thought how the fuck did he know who I was? then he walked over to the table and said, 'go on, go on, and tell me to fuck off, please say something funny,' so I said, 'cockles have gone up!' I'm not that clued up on the Maltese sense of humour, but it was worth a try.

Turned out that he'd married an English girl and they had all my videos, he told me that he lived in a fishing village near Bugibba, I said, 'can you spell it for me? He said, 'no, I can't.' So I said, 'then you should move to Hull, you can spell Hull.' He asked us to go to his home for a bite to eat, so we took his address and went on the Sunday. We ordered a Taxi and when we arrived at his house, bugger me the amount of food laid out was probably visible from the Soyuz Space Station, and there was enough drink to fill a reservoir. The Maltese people are so friendly, and I said, 'you know, if I lived over here with all this food and drink I'd be dead in a month,' then I ate my way through a chicken faster than Dawn French with a custard slice in her hand.

His name was Andrellus, but we called him Andy and it was a bit of a shock to my system when I found out he had three jobs, his main one was on the bin wagon, he went fishing with his father out in a boat, and then also played the drums in a hotel. Big mistake was they all knew I was a comedian, and once people know you're a comedian, they want to hear a load of jokes. It's well known that English is a second language in Malta, but we don't know whether jokes are. The Prime Minister of Malta was called Mintoff, and because at that time, the English government wouldn't pay to keep the armed forces in Valletta, his daughter went to the Houses of Parliament, and threw a big bag of dog shit at our Prime Minister. It was in every national paper, and on the news so, off the top of my head, I said, 'do you think she shouted at the Prime Minister to get back to the sewage farm because there could be a bucket of shit missing?' Well they laughed like fuck. The embarrassing thing for me was that whenever anyone came to Andy's door he would shout, 'this man is famous.'

51. DOWN UNDER

I don't like moths and it's no secret, especially those big ones that look like your mother-in-law's handbag; when I talk about big moths, I automatically associate them with the time we spent in Australia. Perth was our first port of call, one of the most beautiful places on the planet, and probably cleaner than the queen's lavatory seat, so I've been told. It's so picturesque, Perth that is, not the Queen's bog seat, but it probably is. No need for the council to grit the roads here, because they don't have a winter. Our first task was to advertise the show, so they sailed us up to Freemantle, 'there were some friends of yours on here last week,' said the captain of our boat, 'the band Oasis.' That's when the myth went right out of the window, he said, 'they were the nicest bunch of lads he's ever met.' 'They didn't wreck your boat then?' 'No,' he said, 'we had a fantastic day.'

The agent who had booked us was called John Nichols, a proper down to earth Aussie; when you picked the phone up it would be, 'Chubbs?...John!' you had to answer 'John?...Chubbs!' Ritchie?...John!' 'John?...Ritchie!' He sent us a tour guide who was about as useless as a shirt-lifter in a nudist camp, the only thing he told us was that Derek Guyler, who played the janitor in '*Please Sir*', had come out to Australia to work for them, fell in love with Perth and bought a house. Derek, who was an actor, comedian and played the washboard, emigrated to Perth, but unfortunately died, so Derek's love affair with Perth was tragically short-lived.

I said, 'in England, when we talk about Australia, we say down under, do you refer to us as being up an over?' his face never changed, in fact if he had the same miserable fucking mug on his passport photo, they would never let him through an airport check in desk. All of us on the boat got badly burnt that day, but we did experience the Freemantle wind; no it's not what you're thinking, it didn't come out of our arses, pockets of air would come off the sea like very small typhoons almost invisible to the eye. There was a couple about 100 yards away, who'd just erected their deckchairs, when they turned round to get their bags a pocket of wind hit their possessions and threw them 100 feet in the air, and I mean 100 feet, it was frightening.

When we walked into our hotel, who do you think was stood at reception?...Natalie Imbruglia, an actress from *Neighbours* and a very attractive young lady might I add, she also had a hit records in the charts. Now the young lads, horny and a long way from home, who were on our tour had to quickly adjust their trousers to avoid embarrassment, I said, 'if any of you lads go missing I'll know where you'll be, looking through her window or licking her door knob while playing with your own.'

Our show at the Perswood Centre was sold out with nearly two thousand people and went absolutely fantastic. I didn't realise how big Australia was, as the next day we flew to Brisbane and it took us something like eight hours, but then the tight agent had only hired a fucking crop spraying plane to fly us there, not really but it took us so long that at times it felt like it. We went along to the gold coast and walked into the Versace Hotel, which is used by the T. V. company for '*I'm a Celebrity Get Me out of Here*', though we weren't staying there, we'd just gone in to see if we could pinch any towels or ash trays, even though we don't smoke.

Our accommodation was a motel in an area that looked like a jungle, well there were a load of trees anyway, and this is where my earlier reference to the moths comes in, you see my cabin was about six hundred yards from the reception and all the walkways were lit up. On a night time the lights attracted the biggest moths I'd ever seen in my life, they were flying everywhere, and at first I thought they were fucking albatrosses. I'd have been less frightened if Frankenstein had walked out of the bushes, in fact it caused me to have diarrhoea for what must have been four days, which is a fucking long time when you've only got one arse.

The porter mentioned that Gordon Ramsey had stayed there a few weeks earlier, I said, 'did he cook anything without a fuck in it? Because everything he says usually is a fucking this, a fucking that, or a fucking the other.' He laughed, I laughed, and then we danced for a while.

It baffled me why the Australians brought in this no smoking rule saying you can't smoke in any building, because statistically, the Aussies smoke sixty million fags a month, but then they are well known for barbies and surfing, so they probably don't spend much time in buildings anyway. I know one thing, they love jokes, especially about the English; I also learnt that they'll eat any fucking thing, cockroaches, spiders, snakes, stuffed fucking crocodile, etc., and if it's got an orifice they'll fuck it!

52. Hair We Go

A few years ago I started to develop a bald patch at the back of my head and it was getting bigger, the bald patch, not my head and I thought I'd buy a wig, but apparently, I was the only one who couldn't see how fucking funny it was, but maybe it being ginger didn't help. The first wig I got was seven hundred pounds, and felt like it had been woven into my head, but fuck me it was that itchy that I only wore it for two days. Then I was stood in the bathroom with a pair of nail scissors trying to cut it off, but all I accomplished was to make my head look like it had been through a paper shredder. That's when all the sarcasm started with the lads saying, 'What happened there, Roy? Forget where your face was when you were shaving?'...'Did you're lass come on, while you were giving her oral?'...or 'When you get a burger, Chubbs, you're supposed to put the tomato sauce on the bun, not on your fucking head' and so on, and so on...twats!

I realised I had a serious problem down under, so I decided to put the disaster of the wig behind me and on returning from Australia went straight to the hair clinic. At first they created an image to show me how I would look with my new rug, and my first thought was, 'I'm going to look like a cunt, nice bush though.' Then after reading through the prices I thought, fuck me I've already got a bank account with more red on it than black and a girlfriend too, but then I thought a new look might get me more pussy. As I looked in the mirror, I imagined the lack of a decent barnet was making my head look more like the surface of the moon, then I thought a bald head might make me look cool, after all, my old dad did say that head lice were pets, or was it pests? Strange thing is though, we spend hours doing our hair, then when we meet a woman the first thing she does is stare straight at your arse, and so if I did want my girlfriend to run her fingers through my hair, I'd probably have to undue my flies.

What I want to know is why hair stops growing out of the top of your head but comes out of your fucking nose and ears; must be gravity, so I sometimes wonder if God's taking the piss. Paul Daniels wears a wig, and he looks alright I suppose, but then magistrates wear them too, and they look like fucking dickheads; still trying to talk myself into it!

fucking wig

53. Ordinary People

How many times do you hear the olds saying, 'we had no money, but we were happy;' and 'Christmas? All we ever got was an apple, an orange and a small toy.' My answer to that?...'Fuck Orrrrrff!'

Well I'm sure they were right, but that was in their day and I was determined that when I got to that age, I wouldn't be looking back saying the same. Becoming a comic was furthest from my mind when I was young, what I really wanted to be was the world's greatest drummer, and as my motivational dad used to say, 'you've got three chances in life of doing that son, fat chance, no chance, and half a chance, if you're lucky.' Now there's another old saying, 'laugh out loud, and the world will laugh with you!' Well, let me tell you, that's a load of bollocks, as the brilliant Bob Monkhouse once said, 'they all laughed when I said I was going to be a comedian...well, they ain't laughing now!'

You only have to watch the Jeremy Kyle Show, to see real people with major problems, I just don't know why they would want to tell the whole nation about them on television, but I couldn't go on there because I've got all my own teeth. What I like about the Jeremy Kyle Show is that it's not scripted with stacks of well rehearsed ad-libs, everything is said in the heat of the moment, direct from their empty heads, though when the marriage counsellor has to come on wearing a suit of armour then you know there's something seriously wrong. One woman said, 'he gambles all his money, and screams when he wins,' so if he screams during sex, when he's supposed to be thinking of someone else while he's doing it, he's instead dreaming of a win on a fucking one armed bandit. I thought it would make a great comedy sketch if Jeremy Kyle asked me, 'Mr Brown, why did you cheat on your wife?' and I simply replied, 'I wanted to see if all women laughed when they saw my prick,' unfortunately they do!

54. Make 'em Laugh

One day, I was sat my hotel room, I had half a bottle of water beside the bed, and I'd left a 'Please do not Disturb' sign on the door, which is like a red rag to a bull, because everyone reads it, then bangs on your fucking door...twats. When I'm working away, those quiet times are precious to me, because I like looking through the morning papers to see if there are any headlines I can make something funny from. Do you know, I've been in that many hotel rooms it's a wonder they haven't got any towels with my name on.

Not long ago I was asked how you go about writing a joke, well, what I do is if I see a particular situation, for instance, 'man trips up', immediately I might think, why?...were his shoes too big?...was his eyesight poor?...did he have something else on his

mind? So you've already got three variations on the line, 'man trips up', but it's funny in itself how we immediately find someone tripping up so hilarious, must be because we're English. Some gags are instant, as in 'one-liners' and some are long drawn out stories, with these you really need to make the punch line worth waiting for. Whichever it is, the important thing is to write it down and take it in, then if you think of something else about that situation during the day, try it out on some unsuspecting person to see if it creates a reaction; hopefully you'll pick on someone who has a sense of humour, otherwise you're in danger of a good gag never seeing the light of day.

Then of course, delivering the joke is also important, but that tends to come with experience, though if you have a good joke, then it could still get a laugh however you say it, as long as you don't give away the punch line at the beginning. Funny things happen all the time, if it makes you laugh write it down, you can often make a joke out of it later, but if you don't write it down, chances are you won't be able to recollect it.

Although I write every day I do have friends like George, who is helping me with this book. George and I look around for comedy every day of the week, he is quite witty, and also presents me with ideas which I would never have thought about, though he does have a little bit of time on his hands, while he sits in his taxi, most of the time just waiting for a fare.

George once picked up a woman to take her home from a night out, she'd had a few drinks, and when they arrived at their destination, he turned round to collect his fare only to see that his passenger was laid back in her seat with her legs spread and no knickers on. She said, 'I've got no money, you'll have to take your fare out of this,' and pointed directly to her exposed fanny, George asked, 'haven't you got anything smaller?'

I like to think that people can identify with me because I'm a real person who goes through the same trials and tribulations as every working man in this country. If you walk on stage thinking about the money you're going to get then you're not doing your job right, and you'll never make a comedian, the ultimate thing is to be funny. I have an office at home, and on the walls are plaques, awards, tributes; they mean more to me than pounds, shillings and pence ever will.

55. Yer Fucking Joking aren't Yer?

Some of the gags I get away with Now
(By Now, I can get away with Blue fucking Murder)

I was down the gym this morning, pushing, pressing, straining, moaning; no I haven't had a shit for three days.

I was chatting a girl up the other night, she was obviously an animal lover because when I asked her if she wanted to go out the next night, she said she was having a night in with her rabbit.

I call Katie Price, 'Miss Polo', she's the hole with a mint.

My sister calls herself a chicken farmer, because she raises a thousand cocks a year...chicken farmer sounds better than whore.

She's missing two teeth at the front, while giving her boyfriend a blow job, he went over a speed bump, to be fair there's not many regiments can say they've fucked my sister, she's covered in love bites, self-inflicted of course. If she laid on the bed naked, and a vampire came through the window, he'd probably bite the mattress. She's bought my little girl a Rolf Harris doll, you wind it up and it plays with you.

The original Jack the Ripper, was found out to be Polish, wonder which building site he'd been working on.

Rochdale man killed by Hamas rocket, bit off course wasn't it?

Madonna flashes her tits at 56, hope she does it at 60, I live four doors off.

Given two tickets for Kate Bush, don't know who she is, but I'm dying to see her fanny.

Bought the wife a new sat-nav, she's lost it.

Dad went to jail for forgery, I wondered why I stopped getting birthday cards from Cheryl Cole.

Telephone bill £360.00, rang porno line and the girl stuttered.

Wife said, 'my purse is missing, should I ring the police,' I said, 'I wouldn't bother, there's been an aeroplane missing for six months and they haven't found that yet.'

Katie Price says sex is better than drugs, but that all depends on the pusher.

Women who deliver meals on wheels have been caught performing sex acts for extra money, they've changed their name to feels on wheels.

Making a new film about Oscar Pistorius called, 'Silence of the Limbs.'

Richard III was found under a car park in Leicester, he's been find 1,000 gold coins for late payment.

The Chinese have brought out a tablet for addictive gamblers; I'll bet you two to one it doesn't work.

Brad Pitt and Angelina Jolie have adopted so many kids, that when they went to the circus, the clowns came out to see how they all got in the same car without the wheels falling off.

Kate Moss has been cocked more times than Dick Turpin's pistol.

After the death of Keith Harris, Orville said, 'I can't wait for Gary Glitter to be released, because he likes his fist up a birds arse.

Jimmy Saville, Gary Glitter and Stuart Hall walked into a bar in Ireland, and the barman said, 'Fuck me, not "You Tree" again.'

56. TOP OF the POPS

et me tell you about the day I was in the green room at the B.B.C. with Smokie, waiting to do Top of the Pops. Pet Shop Boys were there, the Sugarbabes, and Mick Hucknall of Simply Red. It was Mick's song, '*Fairground*' which stopped us reaching number one; '*Living next door to Alice*' got to number two. After we had to run through all the camera work, I was stood having a cup of tea with Mick Hucknall and for me, personally, it was like winning a Nobel prize; I'd never been that close to anyone who'd shagged so many women before, or surrounded by so many pop stars. It had only been a few weeks earlier that I'd been making a documentary with Zoe Ball, what a beautiful girl she is; I think that's why she married Fat Boy Slim, because he physically reminded her of me. A few weeks later I did a pilot show of a new comedy series for television with Carol Vorderman, so now you know why I wank a lot.

Things were happening for me around that time and I got a part in a T. V. Drama which Stephen Fear directed; he went on to Hollywood and made some fantastic movies. In this drama, they cast me as a mucky, dirty, filthy ticket collector working for the railway, who was interested in giving children pieces of chocolate, but my manager, at the time, said, 'I think we should pull out before the fucking train does, Roy, I don't think this will do you any good at all.' I was still doing cabaret at the same time and we travelled to the Lakeside Country Club. That particular night I had a phone call in my dressing room, and knowing fine well my sound man Aaron was a massive AC/DC fan, I said to him, 'when the shows over, Aaron, we're going for a bite to eat, do you fancy coming with us?' 'Yes, love to.' So, Ritchie, Aaron, Shep, Pete, and I, all went to this Italian restaurant and who's sat there waiting for us, but Brian Johnston, the singer with AC/DC; well Aaron's face. He said, 'you never said anything Chubbs,' I said, 'you'd have only called me a fucking liar anyway, he's a pal.

57. Cakes on a Plane

Now I don't think anybody really likes flying, so when we were coming back from New York, bearing in mind that we are forty thousand feet in the air, and had just finished our meal, this chap got up from a few seats in front of us, came to the door where we were sat because we'd paid for extra leg room, then bangs on the door, takes out a book and starts praying; he was wearing a skull cap so I obviously assumed he was Jewish. A lad sat behind me was wearing wellies, so I obviously assumed he was Irish, said, 'what's he fucking doing?' I said, 'he must think it's the Wailing Wall, he's praying.' He said, if he doesn't sit down, he'll have to pray for a fucking ambulance.' A stewardess came along and asked him politely to sit down, but he just ignored her and carried on nodding backward and forward, by which time a certain amount of anxiety was setting in among the rest of the passengers, in fact quite a few people were worried shitless. The Irishman got out of his seat and approached the Jew, saying, 'if you don't sit down mate, I'm going to fucking knock you out,' again the Jew ignored him, this time pretending to be deaf, which culminated with the Irishman grabbing him by the throat. The pilot came along and intervened by asking everyone to calm down, at which point the stewardess looked at me and said, 'are you ok, do you need anything?' I said, 'I need the bog, pet, but the queue's a mile long, because everybody was shitting themselves.'

Anyway, I'd never seen this before, but to comfort every one after the incident, the pilot ordered the cabin crew to give us some free refreshments, but because we'd been up in the air a long time all that was left was a selection of Swiss Rolls, Jam Doughnuts and Jaffa Cakes, which we all tucked into with glee.

58. Helen Of Roy

'm now coming to the end of my collection of short stories, I thank you wholeheartedly for taking the time out to read them, and now I've chosen to finish off with a personal tribute. Most of the things you've read about so far were about my childhood, youth and earlier adult years, with a few stories about me being a bit more senior, and as unbelievable as they might have seemed, you will have noticed, I'm sure, there have been one or two trials and tribulations along the way, but we survive and live to tell the tale. I now regard my present time as my golden years, being able to entertain as long as I can to a very loyal fanbase, which I again thank you for, it is a vitally important part of my life. But as you might all understand, behind every successful man there's an understanding woman, and family, who help balance the difference between a professional life and a personal existence. I have been so lucky to be in the position where that part of my life has never been better, making me the happiest I've ever been. The person who has made this all happen for me is my wife Helen, to whom I dedicate my last chapter.

I said that I'd never marry again, but then I met my Helen, and my heart leapt. We flew to Las Vegas and spent a few dollars on a cheap ring, but don't worry folks, its cost me a fortune since, although Helen did ask me, 'do you want a pre-nuptial agreement?' I said, 'no, pet, just post-nuptial leg over will do.' So there we were, in the shallow end of the swimming pool at Caesar's Palace, getting it on with no one else around because it was pouring with rain, we were so engrossed that we never even noticed the cameras, because hey, we were in love and it was fabulous.

Before meeting Helen I, was having bouts of loneliness and depression, so I'm sure you can imagine how it was on the day I had to ring her up to tell her, 'sorry darling, but I've got cancer.' It's so hard to accept, when you've just found everything you could ever want in life that it could be cruelly taken away, all sorts go through your mind when you think you're going to die. I imagined Helen going through my office, the workshop as I call it, with its folders, letters and diaries, yes I have shoe boxes full of old photos of bygone days, with photo boxes full of old shoes just to confuse. And it's true, when somebody's been part of your life for such a long time, you start wondering, 'did I tell her I loved her enough, did I spend enough time with her?' We have a beautiful portrait on our stairs of our lovely wedding day; you know she's such an extraordinary woman.

I wished I'd written down every funny thing Helen had ever said, for instance, not long ago I was in a dressing room and rang up to say, 'hi darling, all the tickets have gone, it's a complete sell out,' she said, 'oh that's good, who's on?' Then there was the time I told her I was joining Slimmer's World, she just looked at me, eventually saying, 'why? You'll always have a fat face.' Talk about her having a dry sense of humour, she rang me one day and said, 'do you know what day it is today?' I said, 'yes darling, it's Thursday.' 'Anything special about it?' I said, 'yes, I'm on at Liverpool tonight, should be good.' 'Anything else coming into your mind?' 'No, not really,' then inquisitively she asked, 'can you tell me why

I married a man who forgets their wedding anniversary?' I said, 'I haven't forgotten.' She said, 'in that case you'd better hurry up, the Spar shop closes at eight.'

Did they get that Venus de Milo from Alleycats?

We were sat talking one day about a girl we both know, who's had about five husbands, Helen said, 'do you know, it's a wonder she has any elastic left in her knickers.' I mean she's so loving, I watch her with the kids and the animals, it's like somebody put her on this Earth just to care about everybody, I think she should have been a nurse, but of course when she's ill, maybe with a head ache I get lines like, 'oh, you'll have to get the priest, I think I'm on my way out.' We were watching T. V. Last Saturday, when she started talking, she said, 'it's like sometimes, you don't even know that I exist, or whether I'm here or not.' I said, 'what did you say,

Claire?' she said, 'it's Helen, you bastard!' That's why I love her so much, she just says the daftest things; the dog was sat on the settee and it yawned, she said, 'I don't know what the hell he's got to be tired about.' I know, it's a classic, and there were loads more, only I didn't take my own advice and write them down, I could have wrote a whole new book.

'Aren't My Mates Nice!'

I first saw Roy at the TA club in Gainsborough, Cleveland just after he had been on New Faces. I asked the concert chairman Alan Bell to see if he could get me Chubby's autograph. He did it, and it came back saying, "thanks for asking, Roy Chubby Brown"

I still have it to this day and we have become the best of friends for over 35 years. We have been on numerous holidays together, I have been his best man and we have seen some high points and some low points together. We are always there for each other and I had the honour to work for him for over ten fantastic years. There is no greater man who I'm proud to call my friend. My wife still makes his wonderful stage suits.

We salute you Royston, you are a true legend and godfather to our children Nicola and Peter.

Peter Richardson

I have now been on the road looking after Roy for over 25 years. The question I get asked most is, "How has Roy been so successful and stayed at the top for so long?" Quite simply, Roy was born with a natural gift for comedy, with the ability to find new material every day to keep his show fresh and topical.

There's a side to Roy that most people don't see. It's hard to think of a more caring, generous man whether it's his family, friends, crew, charities and last but by no means least, his fans. No-one gets left out. A true gent in every way. Can I sum up Roy Chubby Brown? Easy, a genious. Can I sum up Roy Vasey? Even easier a true genuine friend. Here's to the next 25 years

Ritchie Hoyle
Tour manager to Roy

Really pleased to have been asked to say a word or two about my mate Roy Chubby Brown. I've known Roy since the 70s when we did the Brewery roadshows together. I was in the Debonaires at the time, we were a comedy vocal band who used to do a spot to back the other acts, we backed Roy nightly as he stormed the clubs. My best memory (and there were 100s) was the night he picked me up by the scruff of the neck and by my arse and threw me like a ragdoll into the corner, I was on top of another artiste punching hell out of him for saying we were shit! Roy heard the commotion and came running in and picked me up, and it calmed down we had a few beers and put the world to rights haha.

Those were hard days and nobody thought, including Roy, that he would have gone to the top where he is today. But through long hard graft I am so proud that he made his mark. He is a one off, but most of all he is the nicest person I have ever met - he is caring and very kind to all around him and puts his private life on hold to help others, that's the kind of person Roy Chubby Brown is... love you mate.

Ronnie Oliver
Friend and fellow comedian

Being part of the show and sharing our friendship has been a true pleasure. Looking forward to many more years.

Being involved in the show with a kind, generous and funny friend has been a cherished pleasure. Long may it continue.

Keith Hammersley
Friend and personal assistant to Roy Chubby Brown

I have been a fan and friend of Roy's for over twenty five years and followed him all over the country

Being from the north east myself I was so lucky to see Roy in his early days learning his craft in the working men's clubs , which alone is one hell of an apprenticeship

To see Roy now and what he had achieved is amazing

He has amazing talent as a musician a writer a comedian

And I'm honoured to be your friend

Steven Lloyd
Roy's publicist